# DEEP Marketing

### How to Discover and Unleash Your Organization's Hidden Strength

### By Bill Hayes

Copyright © 2021 by Bill Hayes

All rights reserved. No part of this book may be reproduced in any form by electronic or mechanical means, including information storage and retrieval systems, without permission in writing from the author, except by a reviewer who may quote brief passages in a review.

Bill Hayes
Founder, Iceberg Marketing Consulting
icebergmc.com

bill@icebergmc.com

*For Nina, Emma, and Sophie.*
*Thank you for your endless patience, love and encouragement.*

# CONTENTS

## PART I
## Broken Marketing

Marketing Malaise .................................................................................... 1
Uncovering the Cause .............................................................................. 27
Seeking a Solution .................................................................................... 37

## PART II
## DEEP Marketing

Discover ..................................................................................................... 51
Discover Your Customer Family .............................................................. 55
Discover Your League of Competitors .................................................... 63
Discover Your Organization ..................................................................... 67
Discover Your Organization's Superpower ............................................. 71
Elaborate .................................................................................................... 79
Embrace ..................................................................................................... 89
Your DEEP Connector .............................................................................. 97
How Your DEEP Connector Will Help You ......................................... 105
Project ...................................................................................................... 115
Using DEEP Marketing in Paid Media Channels ................................. 123
Using DEEP Marketing in Shared and Owned Media Channels ....... 147
Conclusion ............................................................................................... 165

## SPECIAL SECTION
## DEEP Marketing for Start-Ups and Nonprofits

Start-Ups and Young Organizations.................................................171
Nonprofit Organizations....................................................................179

# Preface

## WHO ARE YOU?

- A CEO working to identify why your organization's marketing hasn't been performing as well as you know it should?
- A marketing leader seeking a way to make your organization more competitive?
- An HR leader trying to understand why your marketing team is suffering from such persistently high turnover?
- A board member of a nonprofit organization whose CEO isn't achieving your growth targets?
- An entrepreneur eager to ensure your new business venture succeeds in securing much-needed investment capital?

Whatever has brought you here, you have come to the realization that your organization is facing challenges related to marketing. You'll probably know by now there's no shortage of books, consultants or other resources dedicated to helping fix things. Yet here you are, still looking for the missing key that might unlock the door between you and the success that seems just beyond reach.

Whether found in a book, a website or a blog, the vast majority of advice on improving one's marketing comes in two forms. First, there are lists of best-practice-type measures such as "Top Ten Ways to Fix Your Marketing," or "Marketing Musts for the 2020s." The other form of advice introduces a new perspective: "Marketing and the Micro-Influencer," or "How to Market in a Post-Pandemic World," and so on. In either case, the focus of the advice is largely tactical.

This book takes a different approach.

If the improvement you've been seeking has been eluding you, then it's not likely to be found simply by mimicking the tactics of those who have found success. And it isn't likely to be achieved by fixing the little things. The only way to accomplish elusive improvement is by getting at something deeper—something somewhat hidden. The route to fundamental improvement is forged by asking the same questions over and over in order to identify deep patterns and then to address those patterns holistically.

In my opinion, most marketing books out there offer good, practical advice. So, the million-dollar question is this: "Why are there so many new titles released every year?" Is the advice that the authors offer flawed somehow? Are we all incapable of following their good advice? Does the advice have a limited shelf life?

Why are so many of us still struggling with our marketing?

I believe we are having a hard time successfully applying all of that great advice out there because something structural is causing marketing to short circuit within our organizations. This book describes a decades-long struggle to identify the existence of the short circuit, understand what's causing it, and devise a way to repair it. I share my story and my advice with you so you will enjoy lasting practical use from what I have learned over a long and successful marketing career.

The unique power of this book is that it will show you how to transform your marketing without having to rely on outside "heroes." This book will show you how to take control for yourself and in doing so will increase the value of every other marketing website, book or consulting engagement you have already experienced—or you have yet to experience. If you are really ready to fix your marketing, read and apply the framework offered in this book first. Then apply your other advice. You'll get so much more out of it.

Fixing your marketing means fixing something deeper first.

PART I

# Broken Marketing

THE WORLD OF MARKETING is broken.

My decades-long career has revealed to me that something is preventing many organizations from marketing themselves as effectively as should be expected. And whatever that something is, it's generating a pattern of clearly identifiable symptoms of dysfunction. Further, it appears the source of the trouble is coming from within the organization itself.

If leaders can identify and address what's broken within their organizations, they can eliminate those symptoms of dysfunction and vastly improve their marketing. As a result, their organizations will be able to compete more effectively than ever before.

This is the story of my thirty-year journey to discover what's causing organizations to sabotage their own marketing—and to develop a practical framework designed to correct it.

If your marketing is broken, read on … this may be your fix.

# CHAPTER 1

# Marketing Malaise

THIS BOOK OPENS with a declaration that the world of marketing is broken. While I realize it's a bold statement, I can't think of better way to say it, even though I know that many leaders of organizations—many marketers even—aren't aware that marketing is in the midst of a systemic crisis.

Consider that when people say the healthcare system in the United States is broken, it's something most of us can relate to: the high cost of insurance and treatment, the disparity of care across various segments of our population, declining longevity, and the growing roles of government and big business in managing one's health.

So, while there certainly isn't widespread agreement over how to solve the problems in healthcare, there is a considerable consensus that something is wrong with it. Polling from 2018 showed that nearly three-quarters of Americans believe that our healthcare system is "in a state of crisis" or "has major problems."[1] The key here is that we all know what healthcare is.

On the other hand, the crisis with marketing is very different from the one in healthcare because time has allowed many of us to lose sight of what marketing truly is—and as a consequence, it's nearly impossible to see that the majority of the challenges we struggle with in marketing are but indicators of a much deeper systemic dysfunction.

The only way to understand and eventually correct the dysfunction that's happening in marketing for many organizations is to first examine things at a deeper level … and this first chapter aims to do exactly that.

---

[1] Reinhart, RJ. (2018, February 2). *In the News: Americans' Satisfaction With Their Healthcare.* Gallup. https://news.gallup.com/poll/226607/news-americans-satisfaction-healthcare.aspx

♦ ♦ ♦ ♦

The first challenge in understanding why and how marketing is broken is that marketing isn't an isolated activity. Marketing is a complex array of activities operating within the complex machinery of an organization. Marketing should be viewed as a system operating within another system.

It helps here to think about how the human body works. There are about a dozen different systems in the human body—the circulatory system, digestive system, nervous system, and so on. Each system has its own clearly defined functions and the systems all interact in an orderly, but very complex, manner. Breakdowns, when they occur, can appear within a single system or across a number of systems.

Consider the human circulatory system. Consisting of the heart and the various vessels that move blood throughout the body, the circulatory system is a fairly discrete system with a specific function—to deliver oxygen and nutrients to the rest of the body. If the circulatory system malfunctions, however slightly, the problem won't stay contained exclusively within the circulatory system. The more serious problem is that other systems will begin to suffer or even fail. The muscular system needs oxygen and nutrients. The skeletal system does, as well. Indeed, the entire human body will begin to malfunction.

In fact, the way that people usually discover they have a problem with their circulatory system is that they experience an overall sense of malaise, or feel *something* just isn't right. Something about their well-being is suffering but they don't know exactly why until they seek help and discover the root cause for their illness.

The situation with marketing is similar. Marketing, when viewed strictly as a standalone system, may not appear to be broken. After all, the leaders of some organizations are quite satisfied with how well their marketing is performing. Yet it certainly appears that the way marketing is functioning within many organizations has gone awry and as a result, those organizations themselves are suffering.

Let's think a bit more about systems and how they function. In a broad sense, a system consists of various components working in a coordinated manner toward a specific, larger purpose. In an effective system, each com-

*Marketing Malaise*

ponent has a role and the various roles are understood universally by the other components.

Similarly, organizations—being systems themselves—are designed in part to provide a shared understanding of roles. Organizational charts and job descriptions very clearly describe roles even when those roles are vacant. Role clarity helps us understand one another's function and in doing so helps us understand how we are meant to work together, where we are going, and what success will look like. Role clarity is one of the cornerstones of smooth communication and effective organizational management.

Lastly, role clarity, if it's to function correctly, must extend throughout the entire system. For example, a shared role definition for HR is one the majority of staff and everyone at the leadership table subscribes to—HR, Finance, External Relations, Marketing, IT—you name it. Role clarity requires consensus.

Remarkably, there is one professional area that lacks a shared role definition in many, if not most, organizations—and it's the entire field of marketing. My hypothesis is that this is causing a crippling disconnect between marketers and non-marketers within organizations.

As a career marketer, this intra-organizational disconnect is something I have personally experienced countless times. For example, working with C-suite leaders who were marketers was always so much more efficient. We possessed a shared vocabulary and a shared understanding of how marketing should function, and results were typically positive.

Working with non-marketing leaders, on the other hand, was fraught with challenges. Budgets were questioned. Tactics were questioned. Creative was questioned. Now, questions aren't a bad thing. We should welcome them. Questions encourage rigor. Questions can spur improvement. But more often than not, these questions seemed to be less about rigor and clarification, and more about … pushback.

Further, I began to realize that what I was perceiving as pushback was not isolated. The pushback would ebb and surge depending on what? … I wasn't sure. It felt like while I, the marketer, was doing all I could to orchestrate a successful season (forgive the sports metaphor), the non-marketing leaders saw marketing's role as limited to: (a) designing the team's uniforms, and (b) creating ads that the leaders would like. Everything I had been taught about marketing very clearly described its role as being far more comprehensive and nuanced than what the majority of my leaders seemed to believe.

What was going on?

For many leaders, my duties as a marketer were set forth as follows: "Here is your expense budget. Now, put together a promotional plan that will increase our revenue." So, off I went to build and execute a plan designed to do just that—increase engagement and revenue. But as I built and worked toward implementation of the plan, things were picked apart:

- Why are we spending so much on creative development?
- Why are we spending so much on outdoor advertising?
- Why aren't our ads 'making the ask'?
- Why is our logo so small?

Now, as mentioned earlier, these simply are questions. And they aren't necessarily bad questions. But I realized that although I was initially hearing them as questions, they weren't posed as questions seeking answers. They were actually directions. Notice the difference:

| Questions | Directions |
| --- | --- |
| "Why are we spending so much on creative development?" | "Spend less on creative development. We need media, not creative." |
| "Why are we spending so much on outdoor advertising?" | "I personally don't like outdoor advertising, so remove it from the plan." |
| "Why aren't we 'making the ask'?" | "Rewrite the ad to say, 'We have great stuff. Buy it right now.'" |
| "Why isn't our logo bigger?" | "Make our logo huge or no one will even know it's an ad for us." |

## Marketing Malaise

The persistent pushback I was confronting was causing me to wonder if there was something deeper going on. Perhaps the steady state of tension wasn't a dynamic I alone was experiencing as a marketing professional. Sure enough, through routine professional networking, I began to discover that these frustrations were being widely experienced by most of my colleagues.

As I came to realize that this internal friction in marketing seemed to exist beyond my own personal experience, I began spending more time considering the problem. I would think about it at home, at night, while on a run, and on the weekends. I didn't devote a lot of time to considering the problem in a macro sense, though. My focus was trained upon figuring out how I could help my then-current employer market more successfully. I was early in my career, so I just accepted the situation as a given. In an attempt to address the disconnect as it applied in my corner of the world, I began devoting more of my time to helping others within my organization understand marketing better.

But not for long.

The more I tried, the more indifference I met. And the issue wasn't that people didn't want to listen to me. The issue was that I was having a hard time waging battle against a problem non-marketers didn't even perceive to be a problem. Non-marketers just weren't interested in hearing about my particular views because in their minds they already knew what marketing was supposed to be. The lack of interest I was encountering was causing me to form the idea that something just wasn't right with marketing, in general. As a naturally curious individual, I was driven to understand everything I could about the problem—and maybe even uncover a way to fix things.

Recall that with complex systems it can be easier to identify external symptoms of dysfunction than it is to identify the underlying causes of dysfunction. So, let's think about the human body one last time. When something isn't working with one of our human systems, we often experience malaise—or a generalized feeling that something is wrong. Our physician then asks us to describe specific symptoms. A deeper understanding of those symptoms can then lead the physician toward the diagnosis of an underlying issue with one of our systems. Even better, the physician can prescribe a plan designed to help us heal the underlying conditions which have been causing the symptoms.

I decided that I, too, would follow the approach of a physician. With the same spirit of diagnosis, I began to look for observable symptoms of dysfunction in marketing. If I could identify and describe a number of symptoms, then perhaps I could see more clearly what was going wrong internally.

## Symptom 1: High Turnover in Marketing

The data on staff turnover rates became my first big eye-opener. According to research from LinkedIn.com,[2] marketing-related positions are the worst when it comes to turnover within organizations (see Figure 1).

*Figure 1*

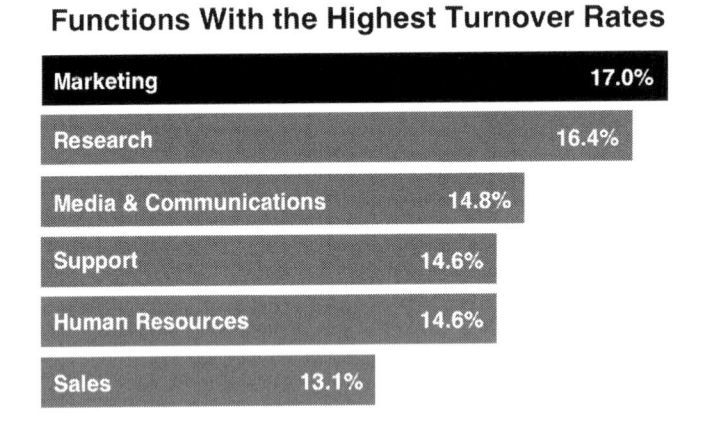

**Functions With the Highest Turnover Rates**

|  |  |
|---|---|
| Marketing | 17.0% |
| Research | 16.4% |
| Media & Communications | 14.8% |
| Support | 14.6% |
| Human Resources | 14.6% |
| Sales | 13.1% |

At first glance, the information conveyed by Figure 1 appears fairly unremarkable. Marketing holds the top position while a number of other professional functions trail behind. However, notice Media and Communications rates third and Sales rates sixth. Media and communications roles are a cate-

---

[2] Booz, Michael. (2018, April 12). *These Are the 5 Types of Jobs with the Most Turnover.* LinkedIn Talent Blog. https://business.linkedin.com/talent-solutions/blog/talent-analytics/2018/these-are-the-5-types-of-jobs-with-the-most-turnover

gory of marketing roles. And while it's true many organizations separate marketing from sales, that separation is an operational convenience. Like media and communications, sales, too, is a marketing function.[3] So, this means marketing-related roles hold two of the top three, and half of the top six spots when it comes to professional turnover.

So, let's now consider whether the high turnover in marketing roles should be a concern. For many, the worst aspect of turnover is the expense. According to research from Gallup, the estimated direct cost of losing and then replacing an employee can range from 50 to 200 percent of that employee's annual salary.[4] I'm quite certain most organizations would prefer using those dollars for actual marketing activities rather than maintaining a revolving door in the marketing department.

And by revolving door, I'm not merely referring to the very costly churn of individuals joining and departing organizations. I also mean a door in the sense that marketing is the vestibule that connects—or seals off—an organization from the world outside.

Consider this: a very limited number of people on the outside of your organization will notice if your head of HR leaves. However, untold numbers of outsiders will notice if your head of marketing leaves. Why? Because as marketing leaders turn over, so, too, do marketing messages. So, too, do campaigns. Whether you realize it or not, your current and potential customers are likely to be witnessing your organization's marketing turnover in the form of a schizophrenic stream of communication and it's likely to be having a negative impact upon your revenue.

Organizational leaders need to be very mindful of this particular revolving door as it is in public view. Losing staff members is part of running any organization. Losing marketing leaders, however, carries an elevated level of reputational risk. Interestingly, the HR profession doesn't seem to recognize it as a systemic problem. Perhaps this is because there is a large supply of mar-

---

[3] Inc. (2020, February 6). *Sales Management*. https://www.inc.com/encyclopedia/sales-management.html

[4] McFeely, S. & Wigert, B. (2019, March 13). *This Fixable Problem Costs U.S. Businesses $1 Trillion*. Gallup. https://www.gallup.com/workplace/247391/fixable-problem-costs-businesses-trillion.aspx

keting and sales professionals and the positions aren't particularly difficult to refill. Whatever the reason, the issue doesn't seem to be hitting anyone's radar.

Excessive turnover in marketing is a symptom of dysfunction that's right here under our noses, yet it's going undetected. Sometimes symptoms of dysfunction don't reveal themselves as symptoms at all. Connecting the dots isn't always an obvious exercise. Still, I wondered, if fixing things in marketing would reduce staff turnover in highly visible marketing roles, then shouldn't organizations be highly motivated to implement that fix?

## Symptom 2: Bad Marketing Everywhere

Another indicator something is seriously wrong in marketing can be seen in the sheer volume of bad creative cluttering our environments. Why is it that so much of the advertising we see in the wild is executed so amateurishly?

It is estimated that about $250 billion was spent on advertising media in the United States in 2019 alone.[5] Organizations commonly allocate about 20 percent of their advertising budgets to creative and production costs while the remaining dollars go directly to media expense. This means the total spent on advertising media, creative and production could be more like $310 billion in 2019. So why on earth do we see so much bad creative when the costs of media and production are so high?

I suppose one could assert we are likely to see a lot of bad *anything* if there's a lot of that thing out there. That is, there's a lot of advertising out there, so we shouldn't be too surprised to see a lot of bad advertising, right? It seems a reasonable question, but it doesn't hold water when you consider that so much of that bad creative suffers from well understood and easily avoidable errors. Let's look a bit deeper.

First of all, what is bad creative? Is it all a matter of personal opinion? I will argue that no, it does not simply come down to a matter of taste. While not everyone would agree on what constitutes good or great advertising, there

---

[5] Guttmann, A. (2021, January 18). *U.S. Advertising Industry - Statistics & Facts.* Statista. https://www.statista.com/topics/979/advertising-in-the-us/

are objective means to identify at least the most egregiously bad creative. Plus, it's not hard to find because there's so much of it.

Let's consider how ads are developed. Most commonly, ads are developed in adherence to a creative brief, which is a concise document outlining the desired goals of an ad or an ad campaign. The creative brief answers questions such as: Who are we talking to, what is the key message, what is the desired result, and what is the call to action? Any well trained marketer will first nail down a creative brief before any specific creative assets are developed.

Creative briefs serve two main purposes. First, it makes good sense to have an outline stating concisely what your creative messaging is intended to achieve. An outline allows designers and copywriters to develop creative ideas while comparing their ideas to the brief to ensure alignment. It's smart practice for organizations to provide a list of requirements before committing to spend their limited dollars on anything. And the creative brief serves as just such a list of requirements for marketing and advertising.

Secondly, creative briefs are designed to enable a client to muster internal buy-in before creative development begins. In other words, the brief is supposed to be approved by all who will be in a position to potentially reject the creative concepts that come further downstream in the process. Agencies take particular care to ensure creative briefs are approved at as high a level as is possible, partly in an effort to avoid the more costly rejections which may spring up later in the design process.

This creative development process has been refined for well over a century. Yet, still, we see so much bad creative in the wild. So, let's now define more specifically what bad creative is. Bad creative can take many forms, but in short, there are three main reasons why an ad could be categorized as bad. These flaws are: (a) content errors, (b) message vagueness, and (c) invisibility.

Let's look at each.

Content errors include ad characteristics such as spelling and grammatical mistakes, links that don't work in digital assets, or missing mandatory elements such as the advertiser's name or logo. We all make errors, but given the high stakes, errors in advertising must at least partly be attributed to a lack of attention to detail—which itself can be caused by lack of adherence to a sound creative brief.

Content errors can create two types of problems. First, and most obviously, those errors result in a situation where potential customers are receiving incorrect information, potentially impeding their ability to engage with your organization. Secondly, those errors can create negative impressions in potential customers. So, not only do content errors miss the mark, they can also inflict damage—and causing damage is the exact opposite of what you are wanting to achieve when paying money for an ad.

The second reason an ad could be categorized as bad is message vagueness. Message vagueness describes a message that just doesn't clearly articulate a purpose. Ads exist to serve a communication purpose. For example:

- This is how our product is going to help you improve your life.
- Here is how you find our product.
- This is why you should click on this link now.

Message vagueness is almost always the result of a lack of clarity in one's creative brief, or lack of adherence to the brief. If your business sells sporting goods, for example, then your ads can't solely make me want new golf clubs. Your ads must be designed to impress upon me that I need to get those clubs at your shop. It doesn't help if the only thing your ad accomplishes is to push me toward your competitor's shop. If your ads suffer from message vagueness, you could very well be spending money to divert business to your competitors.

The third category of bad creative is invisibility. Invisibility describes the degree to which an ad doesn't even make an impression. An advertiser's goal, after all, is to persuade someone to change their thinking or to act in some way—by making a purchase or at least visiting a website, for example. And if an ad is meant to be persuasive, then it must first create a blip on my mental radar.

## Marketing Malaise

In my opinion, invisibility is the most common flaw in advertising. Ads of this type are indiscernible from everyone else's ads and inasmuch may actually be hurting your business. Invisible ads are simply a waste of time and money and there are countless examples of this type. In fact, the advertising industry uses the term, *sea of sameness*, to describe this dynamic.

The sea of sameness describes how so many ads—usually within a specific industry vertical—tend to look so much alike. Think of the ads you see for universities and colleges. The vast majority don't stand out at all from the rest, with the exception of the logos (which, by the way, aren't all that different either). The sea of sameness describes a situation where consumers can't discern a difference between the ads from multiple competitors. And if consumers can't tell the difference between your ad and your competitors' ads, you are almost certainly wasting money.

Plus, it's a lot of money. For example, in 2017, the most recent year for which data are available, degree-granting postsecondary institutions in the United States spent roughly $730 million on advertising—including TV, cable, outdoor, and online ads.[6] Do a quick online search for the term "sea of sameness" and you will discover a wealth of websites and articles acknowledging the sea of sameness effect and describing how important it is to avoid the sea of sameness trap. Ad agencies are keenly aware of the sea of sameness trap as are clients, but there are so very few who are able to wrestle themselves free from the trap.

I'll reiterate here that bad creative isn't simply a waste of money. It can, in many cases, also be damaging to your marketing and to your brand. Bad creative means you are either: (a) pouring money down the drain, or (b) paying money to inflict pain upon your own organization. So, now that we have a clearer sense for what constitutes bad creative and what the costs are—and since we can safely assume marketers, too, are aware of what bad creative is—then why is there so much bad creative?

I think there are two main causes.

---

[6] Vazquez-Martinez, A. & Hansen, M. (2020, May 19). *For-profit colleges drastically outspend competing institutions on advertising.* Brookings. https://www.brookings.edu/blog/brown-center-chalkboard/2020/05/19/for-profit-colleges-advertising/

The first reason for the profusion of bad creative is that clients frequently are unable to articulate a clear message focus and share it with their agency. After all, the easiest way to avoid bad creative (at least as defined here) is first to specify a clear message purpose, and then to communicate that message in a way considered likely to trigger a desired action. I'm therefore tempted to conclude there is something impeding the ability of clients to provide their agencies with that all-important message clarity.

Clients know clarity is critical. Agencies, too, know clarity is critical. But somehow that clarity is persistently lacking. To me, this is a clear symptom something is malfunctioning in the world of marketing.

The second reason there is so much bad creative out in the wild is that creative ideas are often developed and then altered or rejected at the last minute by non-marketing approvers. I call the process, *creative derailment* and it has certainly happened to me. Here is what happens: a creative brief is approved by the marketing team and by the CEO. Creative concepts are developed, and then right before final approval, a Chief Financial Officer (CFO) or board member (or for a real-life example, a CEO's girlfriend) doesn't "like" the new creative concept upon seeing it for the first time. Regrettably—and wastefully—the creative team is sent back to the drawing board.

Creative derailment is a dynamic that has become quite well understood. Regardless, even decades into my career I worried that creative derailment would rear its ugly head every single time I was preparing to secure final approval for creative assets. The road leading to good creative is clearly indicated on the marketer's map, but the road inexplicably and all too frequently seems to be interrupted by unexpected detours.

So, as we found to be the case with high turnover, bad creative appears to be a second widespread symptom indicating something is broken with respect to marketing.

## Symptom 3: Lack of Message Clarity Among Staff

Here's a quick test you can apply to see whether your organization suffers from a third symptom of marketing dysfunction—a problem I call *message muddle*.

## Marketing Malaise

1. Don't give yourself any longer than a few seconds to begin writing down your response.
2. Now, describe in one sentence why someone should become a customer of your organization.
3. Ask the same question of several other people in your organization, and then compare your responses.

    I hope everyone in your organization is aligned tightly on this but don't be too surprised if your answers vary widely because that's the case for most organizations. I have often been shocked by the utter lack of consistency when it comes to how employees talk about their organizations. And it just doesn't make logical sense.

    If marketing is largely about communicating value to potential customers, and if communication can be quite costly, then shouldn't it be expected that all marketers and organizational leaders would pursue the obvious and cost-free step of ensuring their staff members all know how to communicate purposefully about their organization's value?

    Face it, we talk about our work all of the time. We talk about work at social functions, at our kids' soccer games and at the dentist's office. So, why not arm employees with an easy way to share the great things their organization does? How are we all mismanaging this free and seemingly easy step? I'm not sure exactly why but I have observed that many leaders refuse to acknowledge this is a problem at all. Those leaders can have an even harder time accepting responsibility for the problem. In fact, the problem is often pinned directly upon the staff members themselves.

    It was a very rude awakening for me when in a new marketing role many years ago, my messaging was called into question. I mean, as a marketer, shouldn't I know what sets my organization apart? I most certainly should. But it's an organization's responsibility to provide these basic talking points to new employees. It shouldn't be left to new employees to just "figure it out."

    In this particular case, for example, it had taken me only a few short weeks to discover a shocking lack of message consistency among the entire staff—

and among the leadership in particular. What it was that set this organization apart varied radically depending upon whom you were asking.

For example, I asked, "Is diversity an important differentiator for this organization?"

**C-Level Leader 1:**
"Absolutely. Diversity is one of our proudest achievements."

**C-Level Leader 2:**
"Not really. Location and price are what matter the most for us."

**C-Level Leader 3:**
(after pretentiously closing the office door…) "Let's not play up diversity. That's not something that motivates our donors."

Three leaders. Three contradictory messages. And the rest of the organization left to sort out the message for ourselves.

The vast majority of organizations don't do a good job of making their institutional marketing pitch stick with their rank and file, or with their leaders. I have found that in order to make the message stick, and thereby avoid message muddle, the pitch must meet three requirements (which we will examine in greater detail in Part 2 of this book).

In order to be effective, a marketing pitch or elevator speech must be: (a) meaningful, (b) motivating, and (c) memorable. Without a pitch offering those three qualities, an organization—at best—misses a great opportunity. At worst, a lack of messaging consistency can seriously damage an organization, especially if that messaging is coming from leadership or from customer-facing staff.

I like to think of it this way. From the moment a potential customer reaches out to your organization, a countdown clock begins. As that clock ticks, your team has a precious and narrow window within which to establish a purposeful dialogue with that potential customer. Before the clock winds down to zero, your organization must communicate with precision in order to convert that prospective customer into an actual customer. Unfortunately, the individual members of organizations are rarely armed with the purposeful and consistent messaging these moments require, thereby extinguishing many of their organization's brightest opportunities for sales and revenue.

Fixing the problem of message muddle is a task very worthy of being pursued but I firmly believe it can only be achieved via an institutional effort. It's hard enough to craft the right message but getting that message to stick represents an even more difficult task. A workshop or one-off email from the CEO simply won't be enough to get the job done. So, as we found with the remarkably high turnover and as we've seen with the plethora of bad creative, message muddle serves as a third red flag that something is fundamentally broken in marketing.

## Symptom 4: Marketing's Surrender to Big Data

The fourth and final symptom is a more recent development and it relates to what I call the *surrender to big data*. Marketers are increasingly surrendering control of their marketing activities to big data and artificial intelligence (AI). This trend is alarming for two reasons:

1. After having been given free rein, big data and AI in the major social media platforms have evolved in a way that is inflicting harm upon its users. As big data and AI are similarly being given free rein in search and ad serving platforms, organizations are exposing themselves to similar risk of harm.
2. The mechanistic allure that big data offers is causing organizations to overinvest in trackable end-of-funnel tactics and underinvest in the upper part of their conversion funnels.

In order to clearly understand this emergent but serious symptom, we will first look at the role of big data and AI in the rise of the social networks. We will then turn our focus to the paid search platforms.

## Big Data and AI in the Rise of the Social Networks

The surrender to big data and artificial intelligence in our personal lives via the social networks is clearly damaging our social fabric. According to research conducted by the **PEW** Research Center in late 2020, 64 percent of Americans say social media have a mostly negative effect on the way things are going in the United States today.[7] While there is a degree of difference between the opinions of Democrats and Republicans, majorities in both groups agree that social media is exerting a mostly negative influence on life in America. And while the majority of us are becoming increasingly aware of the dysfunction, we aren't having a lot of success coming up with solutions.

How is it that we have found ourselves in this toxic and codependent relationship with "information"?

Throughout our history, humans have been seekers of information about the world beyond what we could see and hear directly. Initially, such information would have come in the form of interacting directly with outsiders. As time passed and new forms of communication emerged (written language, books, newspapers, radio, television, the internet), people gained access to ever greater quantities and varieties of information.

Much of that newfound information would have been accurate, and much of it would not. Similarly, while much of the information would have been distributed in order to enlighten, much would have been distributed to serve nefarious motives. In any case, humans were steadily gaining access to an ever-widening river of information and points of view.

In a stark reversal, today we find ourselves in a world where smart devices, social media, and online social commentary are restricting the flow of that river of information. The type and tone of information we receive via these new platforms are continually narrowing rather than widening. The volume

---

[7] Auxier, B. (2020, October 15). *64% of Americans say social media have a mostly negative effect on the way things are going in the U.S. today.* Pew Research Center. https://www.pewresearch.org/fact-tank/2020/10/15/64-of-americans-say-social-media-have-a-mostly-negative-effect-on-the-way-things-are-going-in-the-u-s-today/

*Marketing Malaise*

of information continues to increase, but it is being channeled through a narrower opening. In a way, the flow of information today is feeling more like a hose with the nozzle being pinched. The narrower opening forces the water to come at us as a jet rather than a navigable river. And it's largely thanks to big data.

So, what is big data and how is it responsible for this trend? Big data simply refers to computing's relatively newfound capability to process enormous data sets in real time and in ways enabling nuanced forms of analysis such as predictive modeling. The social and search networks are the primary generators and owners of these types of big data sets but "big" isn't really the right word, in my opinion. It is said that 90 percent of the world's data has been produced in the last two years—due largely to the social and search networks and our mobile devices.[8] Big data is big like the Sun is big.

Our mobile devices and the social and search networks are designed in large part to enable advertisers to target ads and other content to users on a highly personalized level. We are all tracked whenever we use our devices at home or at work, or in our cars, or on vacation, or while lying awake sleeplessly in bed. The technology is there to help us, and it certainly does in many important ways—but it also tracks us and makes that information available to advertisers.

Now, to a marketer, the sophisticated targeting these platforms offer can be downright thrilling. Digital marketing tools allow organizations to be more selective than ever with their communication targeting. However, the way it all works has a less thrilling side. The big data algorithms box us users into categories. When we engage with content that is served to us, and when we follow or respond to others online, the parameters that define our online selves become more sharply defined. Ironically, as the platforms learn more about our online behaviors, our individual pigeon holes don't become more spacious, they become more confining.

The downside of all this isn't simply that we are consuming an ever-greater stream of information that advertisers are aiming specifically at us.

---

[8] Bradshaw, L. (n.d.) *Big Data and What it Means.* U.S. Chamber of Commerce Foundation. Retrieved June 16, 2021, from https://www.uschamberfoundation.org/bhq/big-data-and-what-it-means

And the harm isn't only that we are being placed into deeper cubbies. The more troublesome manner of harm is those targeting mechanisms are wide open to being used by individuals or organizations for nefarious motives. Unprincipled "advertisers" can, more easily than ever in our history, pepper us with falsehoods disguised quite convincingly as facts.

And not only can they lie, they are lying all day long. Facebook reports that since 2019 they have been deleting anywhere between 1.1 and 2.2 billion fake Facebook accounts every 3 months.[9] That's right, billions of fake accounts every year. And they certainly aren't catching all of the fake accounts.

Such a massive number of fake accounts indicates a similarly massive effort to manipulate or misinform. Whether the effort to misinform is coming from a smaller number of highly sophisticated and deep-pocketed players or whether it's coming from a massive number of smaller players, there's no way of avoiding the simple fact that there is a tremendous amount of subterfuge afoot. And as each year rolls by, it's becoming more difficult to tell outright lies from truths no matter what your political or personal beliefs are.

The dynamics are subtle, but drop by drop, we are each being drowned in our own highly personalized information isolation tanks.

Over the years, the networks have gathered so much data on their users that they are now able to leverage their big data to enable predictive modeling. AI is used to identify signals that enable the social networks to deliver individualized content deemed likely to keep a user engaged and online. It makes sense that the social networks want their users to stay online as long as possible. Keeping users online means more ad revenue. So, the social networks use big data to serve you content that will make you a more lucrative asset. And, for the most part, they don't care what the content is. If the content keeps you online, then everything else is secondary.

---

[9] *Global number of fake accounts taken action on by Facebook from 4th quarter 2017 to 1st quarter 2021.* (2021, May 1). Statista. https://www.statista.com/statistics/1013474/facebook-fake-account-removal-quarter/

*Marketing Malaise*

From a purely mechanical perspective this all seems reasonable. The social networks are only trying to make money, which they are certainly entitled to do. The problem is by relying so heavily on big data and AI, there is no one in control. The unfortunate—though not entirely unpredictable—result is that big data and AI in social media has enabled antisocial forces to shape and even dominate their platforms. Worse yet, the social networks don't seem to have good answers in terms of how to disrupt the hostile takeover.

So, the big question becomes this: Does it make sense that we sit back and allow our organizations to be led down a similarly detrimental path? In order to answer the question, we'll now need to examine the rapidly growing role the search engines are playing in marketing.

## Big Data and AI in the Rise of Paid Search

Paid search has reshaped the world of marketing. Namely, organizations have completely restructured their advertising budgets so that paid search is now the largest media category in terms of dollars spent.[10] Given its meteoric rise, it seems quite reasonable to ask whether the advent of paid search has made everyone's marketing better than it was before. Is your organization setting sales records thanks entirely to paid search? For many, the answer may be an easy "No." For some, the answer may be a resounding "Yes." But for the majority, the bottom-line impact is far from clear.

What is clear, though, is that the organizations benefiting the most from paid search are the search engine companies themselves and the myriad other organizations tied into the paid search ecosystem. There have been plenty of winners and losers on the battlefield of the search engine results page but paid search hasn't moved the needle in a positive direction in terms of how well marketing is functioning for the vast majority of organizations. Why is this the case?

The state of affairs begins to make sense when you realize paid search is structured to favor only a very few. It is well documented that the search engine results pages offer a severely limited amount of valuable digital real es-

---

[10] *US Online Media Spend in 2019 and the Outlook for 2020*. (2020, February 5). Marketing Charts. https://www.marketingcharts.com/advertising-trends/spending-and-spenders-111801

tate. The top handful of positions on any results page are worth gold while the remaining millions of results are worth next to nothing. Our organizations all fight valiantly for those top few positions but 99-plus percent of our listings never see the light of day in the vast no man's land of pages two through 2,000,000. In this sense, the search engine companies' key achievement has been to perfect a way to siphon our marketing dollars from all the other media channels. So, how have they accomplished this?

I propose that the near-unbridled growth of paid search is due to a couple of dynamics. First, we all love to see data. CEOs and CFOs really love to see data. This is true particularly when it comes to marketing data because: (a) tracking and accurately quantifying the discrete impact of individual tactics is almost impossibly complex, and (b) there remains a persistent belief in the saying that "half of one's advertising dollars are a waste, but no one knows which half." We can all understand the desire to know which marketing dollars work and which ones don't. And, after all, paid search allows you to track costs per click, click-through rates, position on page, and so many other metrics numerically minded people (myself included) love to analyze.

Further, consider the paid search invoice. Compared to an invoice for offline media where you are being billed for "ad units," search invoices look comfortingly familiar in that the billable units—"clicks"—represent engagements. To a lot of people (non-marketers in particular), a click feels like a safer buy than an offline ad, primarily because a click is a real human action and is so neatly measurable. In my experience, I found that CFOs were far less likely to push back against the purchase of a click as opposed to the purchase of an ad. And the lack of pushback creates a kind of vacuum that pulls more dollars toward search.

Over time, the superabundance of paid search metrics has even enabled them to serve as ersatz benchmarks against which next quarter's or next year's marketing performance is measured. Did our cost-per-acquisition drop relative to the prior period? If so, then great work—let's increase our spend there. Did our click-through-rates go up? If not, then let's reduce our spend there.

## Marketing Malaise

How have we all ended up in the business of buying clicks? Largely because its mesmerizing measurability lends paid search a veneer of advantage relative to other media.

The second reason for paid search's growth is that it's relatively new and it is still evolving rapidly. And as is common with transformational commercial breakthroughs, paid search is enjoying a great opening rally. By 2010, paid search was widely viewed as the new big thing. In fact, online and search marketing were seen as such a big thing that it was all given the name, *Marketing 2.0*. In the ensuing decade everyone was opening their checkbooks and jumping on board. Even small organizations that formerly didn't do much marketing at all are now able to run their own paid search campaigns.

But paid search comes with a hidden cost.

Paid search is monetizing our organizations' data in a similar way that the social media platforms have done with our personal data. Consider this: all of the data and metrics that the search engines let you track behind your password-protected analytics accounts are also being consumed and processed by the search engines themselves.

The search engines assert that their prime directive is to serve the best and most relevant results to online searchers, which sounds good in principle. In order to accomplish their directive, the search engines even offer advertisers advice to help achieve their end goal of "the most relevant results." In following their advice, however, organizations are highly constrained with respect to what to say, how to say it, and how to optimize their websites to conform to the "most relevant results" credo.

So, let's think again about the fundamental purpose of marketing, which is to facilitate exchanges between our organizations and those who will benefit from what our organizations offer. And let's compare this with the purpose of the big data-driven platforms, which is to make money by facilitating connections between users and advertisers. For the most part, these two purposes align quite well. Organizations want to connect with customers, and the big platforms want the same thing.

But the overwhelming complexity of big data is slowly forcing us to rely on the networks themselves to manage decisions on behalf of our organizations. Google, for example, offers and encourages us to use tools letting them automate our ad bidding for us. Why is there a need for automated bidding? Because there is so incredibly much data to process. Unless your organization employs its own team of data scientists, then managing a manual bidding process can be quite complex indeed. If you wish to improve the efficiency of your ad bidding, then you can either hire the aforementioned team of data scientists, or an excellent digital agency (the usual route) … or you can have Google do your bidding for you. Consequently, more and more organizations are relinquishing control of their bidding to the search engines. Many paid agencies, too, are employing automated bidding. Which all means that marketers are surrendering to big data.

Now, why do I choose to call this a surrender? If Google can be more efficient than your organization can be, why not let them handle it? After all, if the key value of AI and big data is its ability to identify actionable signals in massive data sets, then why not let Google use it to make decisions determining how our marketing dollars are spent?

Here is why.

Those data sets and signals are susceptible to being influenced by the same types of nefarious forces that have caused the social networks to now be viewed as a mostly negative element in society. As such, marketers are slowly handing their marketing over to search engines that don't *care* about anything but generating clicks (money).

The big data platforms don't understand our organizations and they don't understand our organizations' needs. They simply own unfathomable amounts of data—our data. And our continued reliance on the networks will move us farther from control over our own marketing. It reminds me too much of the *Lord of the Rings*. We all think we possess power—and we're all

## Marketing Malaise

told we have power but there's one ring out there controlling all the other rings, including the one on our own finger.

The final question, then, is this. How does the marketing profession's increasing reliance on big data represent a symptom of dysfunction? Is it truly dysfunction or is it just another step in the benign advance of technology? I argue that the trend represents dysfunction because the process of gaining a customer is more like a courtship than a swipe to the right.

Converting a potential customer into an actual customer typically takes a great number of steps and usually a bit of time. The *customer conversion funnel* (see Figure 2) is a useful way of depicting the process because it describes the manner in which potential customers move through a series of phases as they edge ever closer to handing us their money. The first step is awareness, followed by interest, desire, and then action. If our conversion funnel is a multi-step process, then paid search comes into play when customers are in those final one or two steps.

*Figure 2*

**Customer Conversion Funnel**

- Awareness
- Interest
- Desire
- Action

**Paid Search**

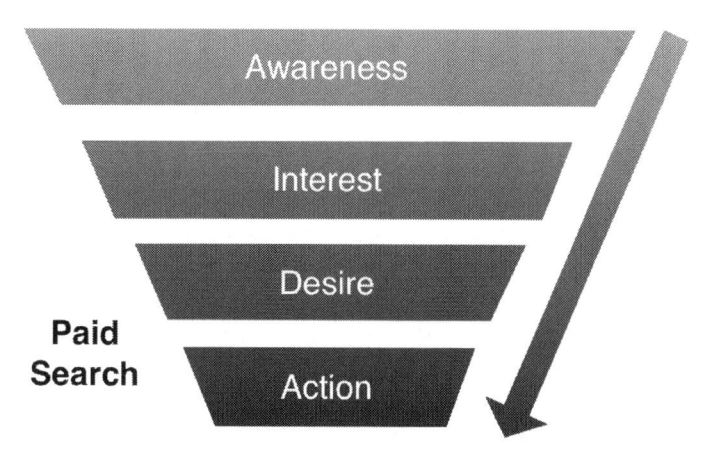

Paid search doesn't help us move potential customers into and through those first few steps, however. If all we ever did was focus on the last few steps, our funnels would dry up. Or, at the very least we would lose a lot of opportunities by engaging only with those who are rather far along their purchasing journey.

In allocating an ever increasing proportion of their budgets to the big data platforms, marketers are yielding to pressure from those within their organizations who favor a mechanistic approach—even if it means turning their backs on the critically important upper parts of our funnels. There must be a balance between upper and lower funnel approaches in marketing. Professional marketers know this, but it can be hard to keep swimming against a current that just keeps getting swifter.

In sum, marketers don't control big data—it controls us. Marketers' willing surrender to big data is: (a) exposing their organizations to risk, and (b) causing them to lose sight of the full funnel approach marketing requires. I therefore believe this trend serves as an emergent and worrisome symptom of dysfunction.

## Can We Discover and Fix What's Causing These Symptoms?

We have now observed and described four discrete symptoms indicating that marketing is malfunctioning. High turnover, poor creative execution, lack of message clarity, and the surrender to big data and AI each pose a very serious challenge for organizations. In combination, the four symptoms represent a massive opportunity for improvement for organizations.

The next logical question—and my next question as I endeavored to make sense of the problem with marketing—was "Can these symptoms and their underlying causes be remedied?"

From my earliest days in marketing, I assumed (and hoped) my professional contributions to the world would come as a marketer bringing value to the organizations where I was employed. But as the decades went by, I began to wonder if my fuller value may eventually be defined more in terms of whether I could help to fix what was wrong with my profession. I have literal-

*Marketing Malaise*

ly spent decades thinking about this problem and trying to figure out how it might be solved.

My first instinct, once I began to think of myself as a marketing fixer, was to help organizations directly as a consultant. But in very little time, I began to consider instead whether I could help larger numbers of organizations all at once.

This led me to my next step, which was to see if I could: (a) articulate the root cause of the dysfunction in marketing, (b) devise a solution to the dysfunction, and (c) share my findings with absolutely anyone who could benefit.

# CHAPTER 2

# Uncovering the Cause

AFTER CLEARLY IDENTIFYING and describing four symptoms of dysfunction in marketing (high turnover, poor creative execution, lack of message clarity, and the surrender to big data), I set out to discover the root of the problem.

## Are Marketers Themselves the Cause of the Problem?

I started by directing my attention toward the usual suspects. Was the problem the marketer? After all, I was experiencing these disconnects personally. Did it mean I was a bad marketer, or that I wasn't persuasive enough with my organizations' leadership? Was there something I could do to make marketing work more effectively?

Upon further reflection, though, my experiences weren't consistently negative. They were a combination of positive and negative, and they seemed to vary rather unpredictably. A great week would be followed by a bad month. A bad week would have an inexplicably great day stuck in the middle. The randomness made me think it may not just be me … or marketers in general.

Most importantly, I was realizing many of my colleagues and successors were experiencing a career narrative strikingly similar to mine. Turnover and frustration were among the most common shared characteristics in our marketing careers. As I gained a fuller understanding of the situation, I identified a pattern I have since come to label as *groundhog day marketing*.

## Groundhog Day Marketing

"Michelle, I need you to fire Dan. We haven't hit our numbers for three straight periods and several board members informed me they don't like the current ad campaign. Let's get a new VP of Marketing on board as quickly as possible."

Conversations like this happen every day. As discussed in Chapter 1, marketing roles suffer the worst turnover in organizations. One of the more intriguing aspects of the turnover is what can happen during the ensuing candidate screening process—where hiring committee members are tacitly encouraged to presume the outgoing VP's work was "the problem."

Think about that ... people with little to no marketing expertise are tasked with selecting their organization's next marketing hero while the predecessor's work and legacy are put up for target practice. I have been through the interview process many times—on both sides of the table—so I speak from experience. These are the types of questions asked during interviews:

- What would you change about the current advertising campaign?
- How would you improve the current website?
- How would you fix the problems we've been experiencing with lead conversion?

Hungry candidates are openly invited, encouraged even, to disparage their predecessor's work in order to impress the interview committee and hopefully secure the position. The successful candidate then continues with the disparagement after beginning in their new role. After all, if negativity resulted in securing the position, then why not continue with it? After another year or maybe a few, the cycle repeats. A star hire leaves out of frustration or is ushered out, and the search begins for next year's superstar. The way I see it, hiring committees are merely looking for their next *former* marketing leader.

I call this process groundhog day marketing because it reminds me of the never-ending cycle of repetition depicted in the classic film, *Groundhog Day*.

Does the turnover process always happen in this manner? Of course not. But does it happen a lot? Does it happen way too much? Absolutely. The numbers show it quite clearly. And what's even more interesting is that turnover in marketing-related roles appears not only to be a symptom of underlying problems in organizations, it may also be causing some of the prob-

*Uncovering the Cause*

lems by creating a groundhog day-like feedback loop. The existence of this feedback loop makes it difficult to discern symptoms from underlying problems. Is poor marketing leading to turnover? Or is turnover the problem that is leading to poor marketing? Or is some other problem causing the turnover?

As the cycle of attributing poor marketing performance to individuals becomes more normalized, we lose our ability to see and understand what's really causing the problems.

## Are Poor Leaders the Cause of the Problem?

Having come to the conclusion that the dysfunction in marketing couldn't be chalked up simply to the performance of marketers, the next among my list of usual suspects were the organizations' leaders themselves. Could poor leadership be the cause? It didn't seem unreasonably far-fetched because we've all seen our share of rather incompetent leaders.

On the other hand, we've probably all been lucky enough to enjoy working with some truly excellent leaders. And a colleague pointed out to me that great leaders can possess different talents. Some leaders are technical geniuses. Others are financial wizards. Others are marketing savants. There's no one right type of leader.

Besides, the marketing disconnect seems to behave more like a web than a chain. That is to say, the disconnect appears to occur across all organizational levels and in all directions. As a marketer, I was just as likely to see eye to eye with a CEO as I was with a colleague in human resources. I was just as likely to routinely disagree with another leader as I was with a colleague in IT. The rift in marketing isn't a purely top-down or bottom-up problem. It feels more random and too pervasive.

In any case, if leaders weren't the source of the problem, I did presume that any potential fix would require a leadership component. Leaders, whether responsible for the problem or not, will need to lead their organizations toward a solution, if there is to be a solution. A fix can't happen without leadership.

## Are Our Current Marketing Models the Cause of the Problem?

Then, many years into my career, something very special helped me to see things in a new light.

I accepted an offer to teach a number of courses at the university level. To me, it was an invigorating opportunity to help bring the science of marketing to life for a group of young adults preparing to launch their careers. Teaching the science of marketing allowed me to share. I was very prepared for that. What I wasn't prepared for was the fact that I would be receiving something of a reeducation myself.

In very little time, I came to re-appreciate the fact that marketing is a remarkably complex science.

Over the years as a professional marketer, I got caught up in the day-to-day grind of managing a marketing department. Most of the time I was focused on tactics, with periodic review of strategies. I imagine we all do it. Routine is what we eat and breathe. And while the occasional diversion into thinking big would feel productive and even exhilarating, doing so didn't align with the demands of the day-to-day. Put simply, my opportunity to stay connected with marketing theory stood in the way of my staying connected with this month's revenue numbers.

Teaching the science of marketing provided me the opportunity to reconnect with many of the models and tools I studied and became enamored with in graduate school. I fell in love with marketing in my twenties because it had the allure of a real-life chess game. My accounting professors encouraged me to pursue a Ph.D. in accounting, but I didn't consider it because accounting didn't fascinate me in the same way. I enjoyed accounting quite a bit. There was a lot of subtlety but it couldn't hold a candle to the depth that marketing represented.

So, when revisiting the models as a teacher myself, it was a rude awakening to suddenly realize my beloved graduate business school version of marketing didn't align all that closely with what I had come to experience and

## Uncovering the Cause

practice in the real world. I shouldn't have been shocked, but the passage of years blurs one's memory.

A colleague of mine is fond of saying that marketing is "part science and part art," which is true. In my view, marketing is a discipline where scientific models provide the framework upon which creativity can bloom. Here are a few marketing models that have stood the test of time:

- Four Ps of Marketing
- Kotler's Five Product Levels
- Boston Consulting Group Matrix
- Porter's Five Forces

These are remarkably useful models that can add depth to one's efforts. The models are built upon the science of business mechanics, but also upon sociology and psychology. Inasmuch, the models deal with the fascinating interplay of communication, human behavior and commerce. That interplay is what makes marketing so challenging. In my opinion, marketers are lucky because we get to work with language, we get to work with complex data, and we get to work with the creative arts. Marketing offers tremendous professional variety and it therefore offers tremendous complexity, which is one reason why there are so many models.

So, I found myself wondering: Could the models themselves be responsible somehow for triggering the disconnect? For example, are the models out of touch with a world that has outgrown them? Are they flawed in some other way? It felt like quite a leap for me to even consider it. And, it just didn't seem reasonable—particularly when one considers that marketers usually rely on several models at once. The models serve as do tools in a carpenter's workshop. If a carpenter builds a house and then that house falls down, we wouldn't conclude the carpenter's tool collection was the problem. In my view, the dominant marketing models aren't culpable for the symptoms of dysfunction we are observing. Applying the models judiciously clearly enhances one's marketing efforts.

However, there is a tremendous depth within the models that makes them at once useful, and simultaneously quite challenging to grasp in all their subtlety. So, is it any wonder that if the models are this complex, it may be too much to expect anyone other than trained marketers to appreciate them fully?

Could it be that the models' complexities made the practice of marketing somewhat abstruse to non-marketers? Perhaps. But then again, that is probably the case for most professional disciplines. I don't understand all the nuances of the human resources profession. I'm certainly not acquainted with the intricacies of corporate finance. Still, it seemed as if there might be a connection.

## We Are All Passive Experts in Marketing

As I continued to think more about how the complexity of marketing may be contributing to its own dysfunction, I had an important revelation. I perceived a dynamic I have chosen to label *passive expertise*.

Passive expertise describes the way we all feel expert in the things we happen to experience with frequency. For example, I've watched a lot of football over the years (though not as much as my brother). Consequently, I feel confident in questioning the calls of coaches or of referees based upon my "knowledge" of the game.

I've never played organized football. I've never coached football. I haven't invested thousands and thousands of hours playing and poring over the details of the game as have professional coaches, players and analysts. Nevertheless, when watching a game, I somehow feel utterly comfortable questioning penalties or play calls.

My expertise in football is, therefore, passive expertise. I'm absolutely not a football expert. But I kind of think and act like one. And I don't even reflect on it. I just run with it. In this respect, marketing is like football. Here's why.

Marketing—unlike accounting, IT or HR—is an activity about which nearly everyone fancies themselves as being knowledgeable. We non-accounting folks are happy to let the finance group do what they do. We don't play Monday morning quarterback regarding journal entries or SEC filings. Nor

*Uncovering the Cause*

do we do so with HR or IT—I'm personally quite happy to let those departments be the experts.

But when it comes to marketing ... everyone has an opinion.

Why? Because the tangible products of marketing communication are so visible. We feel a crush of ads all day long. They are everywhere we turn. We don't even have to turn. They are flashing on our screens, our phones, pouring through our windshields and from our speakers. Everywhere. Consequently, we all feel innately qualified to proclaim which ads are the best and worst, for example, on Super Bowl Sunday.

And the rise of social media has only intensified the volume. Every day, the average American spends more minutes engaging with social media than they do preparing and eating food. Social media is where we look to stay connected with friends, family and the world. It's where we see nephews grow up. It's where we hear about birthdays and graduations. It's where we hear opinions about politics. It's the place where so many of us get most of our information about the world beyond our own direct experience. It's our lens.

Unfortunately, the vast majority of social media users don't understand (or seem to care) that the social networks don't exist to help us connect with our friends, family and the world. Nor do the networks exist to provide transparency and accurate information. The big social networks exist to provide a mechanism through which advertisers can better target us. We users think we're the customer. But with social media platforms, we users are the product. Many people figured this out long before I did. But I still shudder when I think about it.

The point is, the emergent social media ecosystem has transformed marketing and advertising. We are all becoming snow blinded within a blizzard of ads. And we all have become passive experts in marketing.

The twist in all of this is that although we think we can sort the good ads from the chaff, all we can really discern is whether we like an ad or not. The only true way to tell if an ad is good is if it does its job well ... and an ad's job isn't to make us like it. We might detest an ad that happens to be creating sales records for the advertiser. Similarly, we may adore an ad that is literally forcing a company out of business. It just doesn't matter what we like. All that matters is whether an ad achieves the goals the advertiser had in mind.

## Something Within Organizations is Impeding the Effective Implementation of Marketing

While considering this notion of passive expertise, I began to realize that the majority of models informing the professional practice of marketing have something of a built-in blind spot.

I don't have a Ph.D. in marketing. I'm a professional marketer who has endeavored for thirty years to apply the great marketing models our Ph.D.s have developed and shared with us. And while I've had plenty of success in doing so, I've also hit many walls—walls that just aren't mentioned at all in marketing textbooks. Walls that a marketing academic may never encounter.

Another way to consider this is to think of marketing academicians as creators of recipes. Many of the recipes they create are extraordinarily detailed. We are told what ingredients to use, how to combine them, in what order to combine them, how to cook them, what temperature to cook them at, how they should look when they are finished, and so on.

But what the recipe creators don't specify—and couldn't possibly specify—are the wide array of variables existing among us recipe followers. The 350-degree temperature setting for my oven is not the same as the next person's oven. I let my child help me stir the ingredients rather than use an electric mixer. I'm at a higher elevation than most other recipe followers. And when I serve the completed dish, it will be eaten by a set of consumers with their own unique tastes and preferences. The variability of conditions is reflected clearly in the online recipe reviews: "too spicy," "not spicy enough," "too chewy," "not chewy enough," "absolutely love this recipe," "would not recommend," and so on. The recipe, for all its detail, becomes a bit of a crapshoot in the outside world. A lot is left to chance. A whole lot.

Similarly, the creators of our marketing models take it for granted that marketers will be able to apply their models hindered only by the random forces of the marketplace at large. There is no underlying assumption that

*Uncovering the Cause*

the very structure of organizations themselves will impede the free application of the models. After all, why would an academic assume such a thing? In a rational world, their models could be applied without hindrance.

But the world is not rational. And neither are organizations.

It's challenging to run a marketing department when everyone else in the organization is an "expert" in marketing and when plans and tactics can be stopped or altered at any point, and by nearly anyone. Something was dawning on me. This gulf of understanding and expertise that exists between marketers and their non-marketer colleagues may be the one main element triggering the symptoms of dysfunction that we find in marketing.

The insights I have been able to garner as a lifelong practitioner have given me a unique perspective into how marketers struggle on a daily basis to apply science and craft to their utmost value within the perplexing confines of an organization. I don't know, but perhaps it is only someone with decades of practical marketing experience who could perceive these loosely connected dynamics of struggle not as something random, but as something structural.

More importantly, I realized that if the problem were structural as opposed to random, then a solution could be developed.

CHAPTER 3

# Seeking a Solution

IT OCCURRED TO ME that what may be needed in order to bridge the gulf dividing marketers from non-marketers in organizations is a new marketing model designed not for marketers but for organizations—and more specifically, a model designed for the leaders of organizations.

I focus on leaders here because they are the only individuals who have sufficient political clout to even allow an organization to be open to change. More importantly, leaders are the only ones who can commit an organization to carry out change. CEOs or other C-suite members must be willing to embrace change in order for this new model to work. In order to bring about real change, there has to be a commitment. Without commitment, then failure should be expected.

It is important for me to underscore here that my model is not intended to replace or supersede any of our existing marketing models. Our existing models are brilliant and continue to be invaluable to me as a marketer. I use them as a carpenter uses their tools. I use different tools for different needs. But since the model I have in mind is designed to be employed in concert with these other existing tools, I strived to limit the scope of the model in order to keep it focused on one problem.

Specifically, the purpose of my model is to show organizations how to build the internal structure necessary to enable their marketing to function optimally.

I realized, too, if the model were to be effective, it would need to address the damage that passive expertise is inflicting upon marketing. In short, I was hoping my model would enable entire organizations to become more competition-attuned.

## What is Marketing? You May be Surprised.
I say competition-attuned at this point instead of marketing-attuned because I realized the word "marketing" is, in and of itself, a massive part of the problem. And what an irony it is that marketing—the art and science that is (among other things) supposed to be all about effective and persuasive communication—is such a widely misunderstood term. "Marketing" is itself in need of a re-brand.

So, how is marketing misunderstood? First of all, ask yourself (or ask others) what one single word you might use to describe what marketing is. If you are like most people, you might say communication, or promotion, or persuasion, or advertising.

But marketing isn't about communication. It's about competition.

Marketing is about competing for the time and or money of customers, donors and supporters—whether that comes in the form of selling a product or a service, or operating a museum, or running a university. Your organization's existence hinges upon its ability to connect with customers in a world where other organizations are also trying to connect with those very same customers. Unless you have a monopoly, your customers are quite free to choose your competitors' offerings rather than choosing yours. In that very real sense, marketing is absolutely a competition.

Let's look a bit deeper.

Most people associate the term "marketing" simply with external promotion—which is a severely limited view. Marketing is understood by most as the images and/or messaging organizations transmit to the outside world. "External" being the key word here. But let's look at how marketing is de-

## Seeking a Solution

fined. According to the American Marketing Association, marketing is professionally defined as:

> The activity, set of institutions, and processes for <u>creating, communicating, delivering, and exchanging</u> [emphasis added] offerings that have value for customers, clients, partners, and society at large.[11]

On the other hand, the *Oxford Dictionary* defines marketing as:

> The action or business of <u>promoting and selling</u> [emphasis added] products or services, including market research and advertising.

The dictionary definition aligns far more closely with marketing's popular definition. Notice, too, the dictionary definition is much narrower in scope than the professional definition.

The common definition confines "marketing" to promoting, selling, market research and advertising. The professional definition—and the definition to which marketing professors, marketing students and most marketers themselves subscribe—adds product creation and delivery to marketing's scope.

Now, while that difference may seem rather inconsequential to some or most people, it is not. It is a titanic difference. Marketers consider product development and delivery to be part of their scope. This should not be misconstrued to imply that marketers should own those functions on a day-to-day basis. However, it does mean marketing must be involved at the very top in any decision making with respect to product development and delivery.

I can't stress this enough. Marketing models and their students presume that their effectiveness hinges upon having a spot in the cockpit when it comes to the entire scope of fulfilling the needs of customers. A good marketer knows success comes down to much more than just painting the airplane, designing the crew uniforms and creating the ads for an airline. Marketers want to help drive the design of the planes themselves, help inform

---

[11] American Marketing Association. (2017). *Marketing Definitions*. https://www.ama.org/the-definition-of-marketing-what-is-marketing/

and decide which markets are being served, determine ticket pricing, onboard services—everything.

So, whether your organization places product development and delivery within its marketing *department* doesn't change the concrete fact that everything seen, heard, or eventually experienced by your customer is part of your marketing *process*. Marketing is a holistic practice. It must be holistic because marketing comes down to managing the interplay between expectations and reality.

This is why.

Organizations must constantly strive for perfect alignment between the following three phases of the customer relationship:

1. What you promise to a potential customer
2. What the customer experiences at the moment they first contact you
3. What the customer experiences during and after their purchase

If any of one of these three things doesn't align with the rest, then you will end up with either: (a) no sale, or (b) a dissatisfied customer.

When you see the marketing process in these terms, you begin to understand that what you communicate—what you promise—represents the emotional pinnacle of what your organization does. What your organization *says*, in other words, is the most important thing that your organization *does*. Everything else, everything tangible, must align with and deliver upon that promise.

As employees of organizations, we see products being created, and then we see our marketing and sales teams trying to sell those products to customers. Our concrete reality as employees of organizations is that the things we make (or the services we offer) are what come first and what matter most. We make products and marketing's role is to simply go out and sell those products.

*Seeking a Solution*

But this is the exact opposite of the customer's reality. A customer hears our words first. Then—if we are lucky—that customer will experience our product. So, for the customer, our words lead. The product comes second. And the two must absolutely align. The product must fulfill the promise.

Therefore, marketing should be understood as the entire set of activities that ensure alignment between your customers' expectations and reality. The best way to ensure a happy customer base is to:

1. Tell customers how you are going to fix their problem.
2. Provide them with consistent and compelling evidence when they first reach out to you.
3. Deliver upon that promise.

Therefore, it is not just important, it is necessary that a marketing-based framework steer the product itself, its fulfillment, and all communication surrounding the process.

However—and this is a huge however—the vast majority of non-marketers don't see marketing as something so all-encompassing. Ask yourself, "Is this what I thought marketing was?"

## How Organizations Suffer by Restricting the Scope of Marketing

What if your organization provides a service instead of a product? Let's take a brief look at universities, which provide an enlightening example.

Universities in the United States spend three-quarters of a billion dollars per year in commercial advertising.[12] Higher education is an incredibly competitive sector populated with a wide array of institutional types. In general, there are public universities, private nonprofit universities, and private for-

---

[12] Vazquez-Martinez, A. & Hansen, M. (2020, May 19). *For-profit colleges drastically outspend competing institutions on advertising.* Brookings. https://www.brookings.edu/blog/brown-center-chalkboard/2020/05/19/for-profit-colleges-advertising/

profit universities. The vast majority offer business degrees, therefore the vast majority also offer marketing courses.

Now, if you open any university-level *Introduction to Marketing* textbook, you'll see a table of contents that looks something like this:

1. Assess the Marketplace
2. Identify Your Target Market
3. Create Your Product/Service
4. Price Your Product/Service
5. Deliver Your Product/Service (or choose where to make it available)
6. Communicate About and Sell Your Product/Service

Marketing is taught as a holistic framework guiding how an organization engineers and delivers value to its target markets. Many (if not most) universities, on the other hand, see their own marketing department simply as the team managing item six from the list above: "Communicate about and sell your product/service."

One classic marketing model describes the four main marketing activities as Product, Price, Place and Promotion. Like the textbook outline above, the *Four Ps* model constitutes a holistic process placing Promotion as the final item on the list—a list beginning with the Product itself. But we have already seen this is not how marketing is defined according to most people.

Dr. Philip Kotler, widely regarded as the father of modern marketing, knows this well. He states on his website:

> Marketing is a terribly misunderstood subject in business circles and in the public's mind. Companies think that marketing exists to support manufacturing, to get rid of the company's products. The truth is the reverse, that manufacturing exists to support marketing.[13]

---

[13] Kotler Marketing Group. (n.d.) *Dr. Philip Kotler Answers Your Questions on Marketing.* Retrieved July 1, 2021, from https://kotlermarketing.com/phil_questions.shtml

*Seeking a Solution*

In higher education, the notion that marketing should drive curriculum development and delivery (Product and Place from the model above) would generally be considered as either nonsense or heresy. University administrations take it for granted that the academic side of the organization is the sole determiner of how to shape and deploy a curriculum. Consequently, the absence of marketing can be startlingly visible.

Marketing's absence is visible in the way many universities' flagship Product and Place (namely their classroom experience and the manner in which it is delivered) are remarkably similar to those of its competitors. A lecture hall is a lecture hall. And an online learning shell is an online learning shell. Sure, some are newer. Some are larger. But learning environments are remarkably uniform from school to school save for the smattering of logos and banners adorning the periphery.

What an irony it is, then, that while their faculty teach marketing as a holistic practice, the universities themselves limit marketing's purview to only the final step of the process.

It should come as little surprise that in their external promotion, too, universities are largely indistinguishable from one another. We've all seen the ads: a fresh face gazing determinedly into the distance, a stately campus building, something about "Become Your Future," or "Level Up," and so on. Remove the logo from one of these ads, and it would be nearly impossible to identify which university is being marketed. There is an astounding sameness.

The well-documented and aptly named sea of sameness is like an overwhelming force. Universities are not unaware of this sea of sameness. Their marketing agencies tell them they need to break free of the sameness trap, and they repeatedly try, but rarely are they able to break free—much less remain free. The sea wins because university administrations seem unwilling or unable to practice what they teach with respect to marketing.

The fact that even those organizations that *teach* marketing and grant degrees in marketing don't *apply* marketing correctly speaks volumes.

It tells me the disconnect between marketers and non-marketers is profoundly deep. In retrospect, I now realize how very lucky I was to have been able to both teach and work in marketing for universities. Having done so revealed to me there was something fundamentally flawed with marketing. And it served as the turning point when I stopped focusing on the problem and started working on a solution.

Before turning our full attention to a solution, let's take a moment to look at what role marketing should play in organizations.

## How Marketing Should Function in Your Organization

If your organization sells tangible products, it's fairly straightforward: marketing should play a directing role in terms of all the products you deliver. Not simply an advisory role—a directing role. That means product specifications, packaging, naming, everything. If your organization offers a service, marketing will play a parallel role. Marketing should play a directing role in shaping every aspect of the services you offer. To be clear, this doesn't at all imply that your marketing department is running the entire show. An organization is a team with many critical roles. But on that team, marketing needs to be the quarterback and this is why.

Every quarterback needs a team. A quarterback needs someone to throw the ball to. Someone to snap the football. Someone to block—hopefully, a lot of people to block. So, in order to be effective, a quarterback plainly must have a team. On the other hand, a team without a quarterback loses the ball on every snap. Yes, the quarterback has a tremendous responsibility. But the good news for quarterbacks is that they have a team with them every step along the way. And the entire team has a coach—namely, the CEO. As the head coach, CEOs are really running the show. Nevertheless, marketing needs to be seen as your quarterback.

## The Iceberg as a Model

As I considered potential solutions to the marketing disconnect over the decades, two concepts kept cycling into my thinking. One was that I realized most of us had a constricted definition of marketing. In fact, the way

*Seeking a Solution*

most people define marketing is similar to the way we see an iceberg (see Figure 3).

*Figure 3*

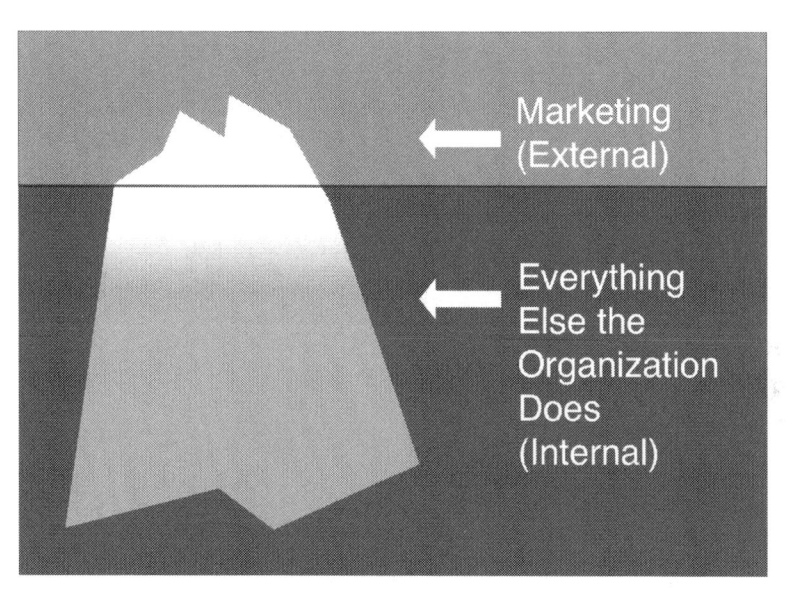

[Iceberg diagram: Marketing (External) above waterline; Everything Else the Organization Does (Internal) below waterline]

We can all see what's above the surface, but most of us are oblivious to the tremendous volume of marketing activity that lies beneath the surface and out of sight. Most people are aware of the tip of the iceberg concept, so the metaphor seemed to be potentially useful. Only ten percent of an iceberg's mass floats above the waterline. Ninety percent lies beneath the surface. And while the portion of an iceberg glimmering above the water is what the world sees, below is where the iceberg's buoyancy resides and where the iceberg's strengths and weaknesses lurk.

Similarly, we should all understand that everything an organization projects out into the world needs to be firmly rooted to a set of core beliefs and values. Most organizations craft mission statements and develop lists of core values to serve as proxies for these core beliefs. But the reality is most organizations don't spend enough time and thought on developing these core elements. Typical mission statements, for example, tend to be overly broad in scope, not specific enough, and lacking in personality.

Many years ago, I attended a presentation by the renowned business strategist, Michael Porter. In his presentation he described how the mission statements of most nonprofits were largely pointless in that they were vague and far too broad. His words really struck me at the time and they continue to resonate strongly.

To me it seems boards and executives believe a good mission is one that allows them to do more. Their idea of a good mission statement is one that offers leeway for the organization to be expansive, and therefore, to potentially grow. The reality, however, is that a good mission statement should force an organization to be more focused—not more expansive. To be clear, I'm not saying mission statements should be designed to limit opportunities. I'm saying mission statements should and can accommodate a high degree of opportunity but only when those growth opportunities align with and enhance the core focus.

A mission statement should serve as the bedrock upon which an organization can build a legacy of good work. An overly general and vague mission statement, to the contrary, provides a foundation made of sand rather than bedrock.

The iceberg model makes good sense here in that the foundational elements of an organization need to be deep and they need to be rock solid. What's below the surface must be able to support the luster of the ice above, while being sturdy enough to sink a ship daring to get too close. Yet, due to a pervasive lack of focus and purpose within many organization's cores, marketers are too often left to develop external messaging that just doesn't connect firmly with anything of substance.

Finally, there is one other extremely valuable aspect to the iceberg model. The model allows us to clearly visualize two distinct, but very important, viewpoints. As a potential customer, the only thing I can see about your organization's "iceberg" is the portion sitting above the waterline. Being an outsider, I can only see your external messaging. When observing the iceberg from this vantage point it is easy to see why messaging becomes the element of greatest importance—the element where the customer journey begins.

*Seeking a Solution*

On the other hand, the majority of people who work within your organization view its own marketing as that relatively small but bright area floating up there above the much larger and more important bulk of the iceberg. When you are working within an organization, you are most likely to be working below the waterline along with ninety percent of the organization. You are physically removed from what the outside world sees. And from your perspective, marketing is a separate area from where you work. In fact, from beneath the waterline, marketing even appears to be somewhat detached from the "real work" of the organization that lies below.

I believe this persistent lack of seeing the entire iceberg as one connected unit is the underlying reason why we are seeing so many symptoms of dysfunction in marketing. When it comes to "marketing," CEOs, boards and staff—most marketers even—focus exclusively upon the visible part of the iceberg. We just aren't looking deep enough.

## Four Phases Framework

While developing the iceberg idea, the second concept that kept cycling into my mind was the sequencing in which marketing processes ought to occur—which is meta-strategic first, and execution-based later. Unfortunately, most of us jump right into execution. I have observed far too frequently in my career that organizations weren't investing nearly enough smart thinking and energy into the internal marketing structure that needs to be built prior to execution and tactics.

For many organizational leaders, marketing is a race. It's a race for market share. A race for quarterly revenue. So, we aim straight for the finish line. But marketing isn't a race. It's an ongoing series of races. And the best way to secure long-term success is to build our fundamentals and prepare ourselves for a long series of victories.

Sequencing is critically important and here's the reason why. As discussed earlier in this chapter, an organization's message represents its emotional pinnacle—especially as far as the outside world is concerned. However, messaging is expensive, messaging is risky, and messaging can make or break your organization. Messaging is a high-stakes activity.

Therefore, in order to shield their investment in these high stakes activities, it just makes sense for organizations to invest heavily in their messaging core before they develop specific messages. An organization's communication tactics must map to strategy. And strategy must map to a core claim describing how an organization is uniquely gifted at helping its customers solve an important problem. Given all this, I aimed to devise a new framework to help us all—marketers and non-marketers—understand marketing as a series of phases culminating in external promotion.

Over the decades, I have refined the framework down to four phases that an organization must undertake in order to correct—and connect—its marketing. Further, the four steps must be taken sequentially in order for marketing to be truly successful. To market successfully, an organization must:

1. Discover its unique purpose in the market
2. Elaborate internally how it uniquely fulfills its purpose
3. Embrace its newly discovered purpose, and then
4. Project its purpose outwardly

I call the process DEEP Marketing. As I was developing the framework, I saw that the four phases formed the acronym, DEEP. Perfect—a word that says it all.

Recall that the purpose of this new model is to extend marketing deeper into the heart of the organization, thereby minimizing the disconnect between marketers and non-marketers, and ultimately enabling the organization to communicate more powerfully and successfully in the external world.

Here is how DEEP Marketing works.

PART II

# DEEP Marketing

CHAPTER 4

# Discover

THE FIRST STEP in DEEP Marketing is a robust discovery process designed to help an organization gain an honest self-assessment along with an assessment of the world in which they operate. Most marketing models include processes akin to these. They usually call this phase market research, or market assessment. In fact, many marketing models focus almost exclusively on this phase. Its value should be apparent.

After all, if we want to compete well, we must study our environment and get to know the forces and the players within it. This step may appear similar to what an organization does when performing a *SWOT* analysis—by compiling a list of its own Strengths and Weaknesses, and of its market's Opportunities and Threats. A *PEST* analysis is similar in that we evaluate the Political, Economic, Social and Technological factors acting as roadblocks or opportunities for our organization. The marketing profession has developed many useful tools to guide us through the market assessment phase.

However.

While I have participated in organizational SWOT and PEST assessments many times in my career, doing so felt too often like an afterthought because the analyses didn't truly inform the strategy that came after. In such cases, I got the sense that the analyses were carried out more to substantiate what the leadership was planning to do anyway. Performing the assessments felt like checking a box. But checking a box is little more than a waste of time. When assessing ourselves and our environment, we must perform our work openly and candidly, even if our discoveries turn out to be a bit inconvenient.

Another common pitfall with traditional market assessments is that we often hear people talk about qualities such as *unique selling propositions* or *distinctive competence*. These two marketing terms are paraded out when organizations try to articulate the clear and concise quality that makes them special. However, these terms assign too much weight to the innate qualities of the organization itself. They don't place sufficient importance upon customer needs or upon the competitive environment.

The marketing scientist in me craved an assessment process offering a fuller context. Over time, I developed a framework specifically designed to describe the marketing environment in a manner that could serve as the foundation for all the later steps in DEEP Marketing. I wanted my model to challenge people's thinking so I opted to avoid familiar two-dimensional concepts like strengths versus weaknesses. I chose instead to describe organizations in terms of the real-world milieus within which they operate.

## The DEEP Marketing Discover Framework

Any organization's marketing environment can be meaningfully described by three constellations:

- The Customer Family
- The League of Competitors
- The Organization Itself

In brief, the *Discover* phase of DEEP Marketing is a process of describing these three constellations and then identifying the sweet spot(s) where the constellations converge advantageously. Identifying these areas of convergence is the most laborious aspect of the DEEP process. It is also the most important aspect because the sweet spot is where we will place our flag and fulfill our destinies. The sweet spot can't be vague. It must be clear. But getting to that clarity requires intentionally allowing things to get a bit blurry first.

We know our eventual goal in the DEEP process is to get very focused and specific. However, this doesn't mean we want to immediately start narrowing

*Discover*

our realm of possibilities. If we are looking for the ideal nexus of these three constellations, then the best way to find it is to expand the three constellations first. Why? Because we want to look at each constellation from every angle possible. We want to look for spaces our competitors won't see easily. Expanding allows us to get more granular, allowing us to find the area(s) where our organizations can build a fortress of strength.

We all hear that finding a needle in a haystack is next to impossible. However, if we could inflate the haystack and move all around and throughout the hay cloud, it would become possible to locate the proverbial needle. In fact, it may be the only way to find it intentionally.

Now, let's take a thorough look at our first constellation: the Customer Family.

# CHAPTER 5

# Discover Your Customer Family

I HAVE CHOSEN the words carefully, so let me explain why I use the term, "customer family." As any good marketer should know, an organization's customer base is not a fixed entity—it is nebulous across many dimensions. Some transactions occur in a moment (for example a hot dog purchased at the ballpark). Some transactions last several days (for example, a stay at a vacation resort). And some endure for decades (for example, a 30-year home mortgage).

Likewise, customer relationships can endure for varying amounts of time. You may be a regular customer at a local coffeehouse where you make brief but daily transactions to support your coffee habit. Or you may make a one-time purchase of coffee at a street fair.

These shades of gray extend backward into the past and forward into the future, as well. In other words, your customer set includes yesterday's customers, today's customers, and future customers. Is your future customer base poised to grow significantly according to demographic trends, for example? If so, your organization may want to focus more resources on them in favor of other customer segments.

The key takeaway is that your customers are not likely to be a neatly defined group. The notion of who your customer is should extend well beyond who your current customers are. We will add clarity by segmenting our audience as we move further into the process. But at this stage, we need to keep the definitions intentionally hazy.

Lastly, transactions typically don't involve just one single customer. We are social animals and we seek, and are influenced by, the input of our friends, family, co-workers, neighbors, and other social circles when making our buying decisions. It is therefore wise to consider each one of our individual customers as a member of a group. We should sell to a social cluster in order to secure the business of each paying customer.

The customer family, therefore, includes:

- Current one-time customers
- Current repeat customers
- Potential customers (prospects, suspects, and competitors' customers)
- Lost customers (former customers who no longer have a need for your product or who have abandoned you for a competitor)
- Family and friends (and other influencers) of your current, repeat, potential and lost customers

Now that we have a clearer idea of whom to include in the customer family, we need to gather insights about them and from them. There are many ways to do this and market research is a well established discipline, so the process of gathering insights doesn't have to be difficult. A market survey is the best place to start.

## How to Build an Actionable Market Survey

A market survey is a research tool designed to help organizations learn about customers' attitudes, preferences, usage patterns, and their awareness of your organization and of your competitors.

All organizations should perform routine market surveys. The data, when analyzed and applied properly, will help you be far more effective with your marketing budget. Now, my experience has been that organizational leaders can be more than a bit reluctant to pay for research every year, thinking of it as more of a once-every-ten-years type of investment. This is unfortunate because organizations should think of the expense as regular maintenance for one's car. You could skip the maintenance and save money this year but you will almost certainly regret it somewhere down the road should you decide to forgo it.

## Discover Your Customer Family

Fortunately, there are many businesses and online resources whose sole purpose is to help organizations like yours conduct market research. And while it can be done internally and on the cheap (if you absolutely must), I highly recommend hiring an outside firm to do your research for you. An outside firm lives and breathes research and will add value you aren't likely to be able to match internally.

In addition, I find it beneficial to employ the services of a research partner with some experience in your particular industry—but not too much. If a firm has done some research in your industry, they will possess pre-existing knowledge that might well improve your own research. On the other hand, I have found that a firm specializing exclusively in your industry may deliver work influenced too heavily by the dictates of your competitors. As a result, your research findings are likely to be uncannily similar to those of your competitors. You really don't want your research to be a repackaged version of someone else's research. I like to go for the middle.

Costs can range anywhere from hundreds of dollars to tens of thousands. And, as with most things, you do tend to get what you pay for. Still, what you really get out of market research is determined more by the amount of time and thought you put into it, than it is by the out-of-pocket cost.

The real value of this section of the book, though, is not to describe how to perform market research, it is about how to make sense of your market research findings, which is the vastly more important and difficult part.

Your market study should be designed to gather the views and beliefs from individuals who are in the market for what your organization offers. Recall that your organization exists either to solve someone's problem or to help someone avoid a potential problem. So, the point of your market survey is to learn all you can about people who are your potential customers. You also want to learn all you can about the problem your organization exists to solve.

Furthermore, it's very important to realize that your customers may not be adept at describing in detail the problem(s) that your organization might potentially solve. By collecting the views of a large number of prospective customers, your research can enable you to identify patterns that may reveal an unarticulated problem or need. If you are able to identify such a problem, then your organization can potentially articulate that need for the prospective customer.

Following are the types of questions you'll want to ask and the information you will want to discover:

- Can they name your organization without being prompted?
- Have they ever heard of your organization, even after you mention its name?
- Do they have any opinions about your organization?
- Can they name any other organizations that offer solutions similar to what your organization offers?
- On some type of scale, how well do you and your competitors solve their problem?
- What does the problem mean to them?
- Does the problem only apply to them? Or are other people, such as family members, impacted as well?
- What pain or inconvenience does the problem cause them?
- How would they feel if the problem were alleviated?
- Where do they live? What's their educational level? Income level? Family characteristics?
- What else can you describe about their behaviors and interests?
- What are their media consumption patterns?

As you can see, there are a lot of data points to collect. Asking the right questions is critically important. This is another reason why I recommend using an outside partner. Market research firms conduct this type of work all the time and are likely to give you great advice. Don't let the partner tell you exactly what you need, though. Let them guide you but ask a lot of questions about the survey before data collection begins.

Here are a few techniques that can add rigor to the survey. Before it goes live, have an associate or friend take the pre-launch survey. Then go through their responses and think about what follow up questions you may have. Can you add any of those questions to the survey? Ask a small group of associates to discuss the survey in a group. Do they all read the questions the same way? Is there anything vague about the questions? The more time you spend fine tuning the survey tool before you deploy it, the more useful the data will be on the other side.

## How to Squeeze Every Bit of Value Out of Your Market Survey

When your data collection and analysis are complete, you will receive a report from your research partner. The report will include an executive summary, a detailed examination of the findings from the survey, and a whole lot of accompanying tables and data. It will probably be a very large document. Unfortunately (or fortunately, depending on your appetite for analysis), the sheer volume of data in the report can be a bit overwhelming. Consequently, many people will just go to the executive summary and call it good.

Please don't be one of those people.

Like wedding photo albums, I have found that most market research executive summaries tend to look a bit too much like everyone else's. The faces are different and the wedding venues may be different but the poses are the same. There's a formula guiding the photographer through the various wedding moments and vignettes but the formula can sometimes dominate. It's difficult to escape the cookie cutter.

Similarly, market research summaries can often lead to cookie-cutter findings, such as: "the three things that matter most to your potential customers are value, quality, and convenience." Unfortunately, too many organizations simply accept executive summary recommendations as gospel—but doing so can be a huge mistake. Do not forget, the key benefit of hiring a pro to do your market research isn't to have them point out the obvious. We all know that people care about value, quality and convenience. There is nothing insightful about that. The point isn't to aggregate findings into sweepingly bland and impractical generalizations.

The point of market research is to look for hidden gems. The point is to discover things you wouldn't otherwise have realized.

So, when you receive your survey results, spend a lot of extra time thinking about the findings. I say this because your market research partner will make a series of high-level findings and recommendations. Their findings will not benefit from the depth of knowledge you have about your organization's niche. Look for areas where the findings seem unusual. Does your organization rate exceptionally high or low in any particular traits? Does your audience skew really heavily in terms of certain values? If so, you may be able to appeal to them in unique and surprising new ways.

## Uncovering Insights About Your Customer Family

Now we know that making sense of research findings requires you to look much deeper than the executive summary. So, let's get more specific. For example, let's say you run a museum and you learn the following things from your market research:

- You rank low relative to your competitors in terms of the percentage of visitors "with children in their party."
- Your visitors "with children in their party" spend more time and money in the gift store and cafe.
- Your visitors "with children in their party" spend less total time at your museum than visitors without children.
- You rank low relative to your competitors in terms of how "child friendly" your museum is.

Okay, one possible direction upon reading these findings would be to market more concertedly toward families with children, since, after all, they

*Discover Your Customer Family*

spend more on average. They appear to be a more lucrative customer segment. Another direction may be to add more child-friendly activities in order to make your museum more appealing to those groups with children.

How should you decide how to react? My advice is: don't react. Yet. The whole point of the Discovery phase in DEEP Marketing is to help you defer on making tactical decisions until you can get a better look at your other two constellations—your league of competitors and your own organization. Why? Because user insights aren't worth a lot until they can be joined with insights about our competitors and ourselves.

I think of it as if I'm putting together a giant jigsaw puzzle that's actually three puzzles which join in some way—but I don't yet know what the final puzzle is supposed to look like and the pieces from the three puzzles are all mixed together. It's a very different process from when you know what the final puzzle is supposed to look like.

So, think about the things you are learning. Let your findings percolate in your mind as you prepare to discover more about your competitive environment and more about your own strengths.

CHAPTER 6

# Discover Your League of Competitors

YOUR LEAGUE of competitors represents the collection of organizations similarly engaged in meeting the needs of your customer family. I use the term "league of competitors" here instead of simply "competitors" because it serves to remind us we are in a competition that's more like a team sport than a running race. We aren't simply attempting to beat everyone to some specified finish line—competition over. We are playing in an ongoing multi-season tournament where we will record wins and losses. And our competitors aren't individuals. They are teams with revolving rosters, as is our team.

So, let's look a bit deeper.

First of all, don't immediately confine your list of competitors to those organizations against which you are currently competing most directly. One well-established way of thinking about competitors is to consider both direct competitors and indirect competitors. If your organization sells books, for example, then your direct competitors are other organizations selling books. Your indirect competitors would include organizations selling things that are substitutes for your product(s). So, TV streaming services would fit in that category because people who buy books for personal entertainment also pay to watch movies for the same entertainment fix. A successful TV streaming service could steal some of the business you are doing with your customer family.

The point is we should adopt an approach here like we did with our customer family. Let's look at another example. If you are a private university offering undergraduate and graduate degrees, then here is a list of the types of organizations you may consider to be in your league of competitors:

- Other private universities offering undergraduate and graduate degrees
- Public universities offering undergraduate and graduate degrees
- Private organizations offering non-degree credentials and certificates
- Online platforms offering non-degree credentials and certificates
- Free online educational resources
- The status quo—or, in other words, deciding not to pursue additional education

As you can see, your list of competitors can be pretty long. Nevertheless, it is important not to rule out any categories too early. While you may be tempted to assume up front that your small university is not competing with the large public universities, for example, you may learn that, as far as your customer family is concerned, you are—at least in certain ways. So, keep things broad for now and we will narrow things down soon.

## Discovering Insights About Your League of Competitors

As was the case with learning about the customer family, we need to conduct some market research to learn more about our competitors. Ideally, you will learn quite a bit about both in the same study. First of all, you will learn how you rank among your competitors—at least in the eyes of your potential customers. Construct your market survey so people can offer their opinions regarding how well your organization performs relative to your competitors on different dimensions, such as quality, customer service, value, price, ease of use, and so on.

It can be very valuable to see how you rank, according to potential customers. But keep in mind these are just external opinions. They are impor-

*Discover Your League of Competitors*

tant, but they are opinions, and not facts. In order to get something closer to facts, you can do your own research by performing a competitive analysis comparing your organization with your competitors.

For example, if your organization offers pet products, you can build a spreadsheet arranging your competitors into rows and placing various product or service dimensions in columns. Those dimensions would include things such as: price for a typical and specific shopping cart of items; proximity to free parking; total retail square footage; typical number of sales clerks; and so on. Then you can start to fill in the data table yourself or you can hire a shopper or an intern to help. You can also discover research online from trade publications or from local business journals where ranked listings frequently can be found. While most organizations find this variety of objective, fill-out-the-spreadsheet research is sufficient when it comes to competitors, it is not.

I have found you can add a great deal of depth to your analysis if you also study your competitors based upon what they are saying about themselves in their own marketing. Look at their ads, look at their website and landing pages. Look at how they portray themselves in their marketing. Are they attempting to project an image of price leadership? Do they portray themselves as number one in quality? Do they portray themselves as having the best customer service?

It is important to realize that what your competitors are saying in their marketing reflects what they have found in their own research. Their words have been chosen either to reinforce what they have found—or to shift perceptions into a direction they desire. Ask these types of questions when reviewing your competitors' advertising and marketing:

- What's their narrative?
- Are they just talking about themselves or are they talking (directly or indirectly) about your organization, too?
- What's their tone?
- Where are their ads being placed?
- How are they performing on search engine results pages?

- Where are you landing when you click on their search listings?
- How directly are they nudging a user toward converting on the website?

Gathering this type of information about your competitors is invaluable in that it allows you to build a detailed perceptual map describing the organizations that are all attempting to solve your customers' problems. Your organization fits upon that map somewhere. And the good news is you can shift where you are located on the map. Depending on your effort, you can shift it a little or even a lot.

On the other hand, the bad news is if you don't pursue your marketing with a clear purpose, your competitors are likely to redraw the map for you, and your organization may get shifted into a direction weakening your market position. Remember, your organization is absolutely involved in a competition. If you aren't purposeful about your direction and your place in the world, others are likely to dictate it for you.

Lastly, look at the words your competitors are using in their taglines. That is where they really boil down their truth. For example, if your organization is in health care products and your competitors are all talking about "staying young" or "turning back the clock," you might explore whether your organization can lean into messaging emphasizing "redefining old."

If you are able to identify a distinguishing concept or even one single but loaded word that sets you apart, then you can potentially embed it in a foundation upon which to build something grand.

CHAPTER 7

# Discover Your Organization

THE THIRD SPHERE you'll need to describe after securing a clearer picture of your customer family and your league of competitors is … yourself. If you've performed a SWOT analysis before, then you'll recognize that this activity focuses on the S and the W, but mostly on the S—your strengths.

The end goal here is to find something (or a few things) that your organization excels at. I have found most organizations tend to have a few traits in their DNA that set them apart from their competitors. The premise is simple. Since we are in a competition, our path toward excellence is either via processes where we improve upon our weaknesses or processes where we build upon our strengths.

On an operational basis, of course we must work on improving our weak areas. So, to be clear, I'm not proposing we ignore our weaknesses. It's just that doing so should be relegated more to an operational level. In this exercise, we are focusing on a meta-strategic level—the level informing all we do. If our primary strategic focus is on fixing our weaknesses, then we just aren't likely to be winning many competitions.

Therefore, I absolutely advocate a strengths-based approach. After all, our strengths are gifts we can share with others. And sharing what we are good at is one of the very cornerstones of the free enterprise system. If I'm gifted at farming and you are gifted at hunting, we each can focus our energies upon what we do best and then trade with each other. This specialization allows us each to enjoy a greater quantity and diversity of food than if we both did our own hunting and farming in isolation.

An organization's strengths usually align with its purpose. Museums, for example, are typically started in order to shepherd a collection at risk of being lost or diminished. Universities are started in order to serve a niche whose educational needs are not being met. Bakeries are started by people who have a talent for creating foods that others want but can't create on their own. Software companies are started by individuals gifted in developing technological solutions to help others solve problems they may not even know they have.

Even deeper than purpose, though, a driving passion frequently informs most any organization's beginnings. *Purpose* is a statement of fact. It describes an end toward which we are working. For example, "Our organization's purpose is to provide the highest quality baked goods to our customers." *Passion*, on the other hand, goes deeper.

Passion describes why you even bother to provide the highest quality baked goods. For example, "Our passion is to make our customers feel as special and loved as we did when our grandmother served us her delicious freshly baked scones, pies and dinner rolls. It's why we get up at 3 a.m. every morning."

An organization's passion is like a flame that mustn't be allowed to die. Or, to put it another way, without such a flame, an organization will often lose its ability to connect with its purpose. But unfortunately, organizations lose touch with their purpose all of the time. What happens is, as time goes by, and as leaders leave and are replaced, it becomes increasingly difficult for an organization to connect with its original passion. The organization's focus begins to shift. New employees join the organization and fall out of step with other employees.

One reason for this is that new employees form a special bond with an organization during their first days and months. What comes across as the organization's focus during those first few months will, by default, become the employee's flame. Eventually, the organization will house an assortment of flames. Staff will be working toward somewhat differing purposes. Obviously, this is not an ideal situation.

The DEEP Marketing process is designed, among other things, to help organizations reconnect with their passion and to give their purpose a firmer foothold because an organization that celebrates and shares its unique gifts is better prepared to succeed.

## Discovering Insights About Your Organization

So, how do we begin to sketch an accurate picture of our organization's identity? There are two main steps. The first step is to identify some of the organization's key strengths. The second step is to validate those strengths. It all begins by talking with and listening to people from throughout the organization.

You will want to ask:

- What do you think sets our organization apart from the competition?
- What makes our organization invaluable to its customers?

Ask as many people as you can: C-suite leaders, front line workers, support staff, board members, and current customers.

The reason you want to gather the input from as many people as possible is in order to get a feel for whether the things you hear are universal or random. For example, you may hear one thing repeated over and over. Ideally you will begin to get a feeling for there being a dominant idea or two. The second reason you want to ask a lot of people is that you never know where your most brilliant insights will come from.

We would all like to think that the great ideas come from the people who are being paid the most, but it's certainly not always the case. Very often you will get great insights from your front-line staff, which makes perfect sense, since they are dealing with customers all the time. Do not fail to include your customer-facing staff in this process.

After you've gathered input, you will need to do some validation of your findings. For example, if you are hearing that your organization's secret sauce is in how insanely well it serves its customers, then you will want to gather data in order to validate whether customer service is really all that great. The point here is we aren't just trying to find out what people think the organization is good at. We are also attempting to find out what the organization objectively is good at.

Far too many organizations pride themselves on being excellent at things where they don't truly excel. Candor is critically important during this phase. The entire point of the exercise is to discover truths, not to perpetuate half-truths or false narratives.

So, how does one obtain objective validation of one's findings about the organization? I recommend relying on third-party data wherever possible. The goal is to be able to communicate very succinctly and powerfully that your organization is really good at [fill in the blank]. In my opinion, there is nothing more powerful than a simple statement of fact to do just that.

If your analysis leads you to believe that your organization is gifted at product quality, then you need to be able to say it concretely. For example:

- Our products last three times longer than our competitors' products
- 75 percent of experts choose our products over our competitors' products
- Maintenance costs on our products are 50 percent lower than for our competitors' products

Another great reason to rely on external data is that it can make your organization look so much more credible. We see it being done all the time, right?

- 4 out of 5 dentists recommend …
- Best truck for three years in a row according to …
- Top-ranked university according to …

By linking your organization's key strength(s) with a concise declarative fact, you gain a meaningful differentiator. In addition (as we will see in Chapter 12), you will gain a new family of metrics against which your organization can monitor its ongoing performance.

CHAPTER 8

# Discover Your Organization's Superpower

THUS FAR, we have completed an analysis of the three constellations that together describe the environment in which our organization competes. In the process, we have attempted to expand those constellations and add as much detail as possible in order to identify a nexus, or a sweet spot, where the constellations align advantageously.

I refer to this sweet spot as an organization's superpower. Superpowers, though, are surprisingly complex. Superpowers aren't absolute—their potency is determined by a number of environmental factors.

For example, Superman is the epitome of what it means to possess superpowers. He can fly, he can move buildings, and he can see through things. However, Superman's powers aren't superpowers at all when he's on his birth planet of Krypton. His abilities on that planet are the same as everyone else there. Similarly, when exposed to kryptonite, Superman's powers fade. When in the presence of villains who possess their own superpowers, Superman's powers are, again, checked. So, Superman's powers aren't absolute. They are shaped by three familiar factors: (a) his unique capabilities, (b) the environment in which he finds himself, and (c) the presence of other players who possess their own superpowers.

Most importantly though, a superpower can't truly be considered a superpower unless it meets a need or alleviates some form of pain. If Superman used his powers only in order to win sporting events, he wouldn't be meeting anyone else's needs. Our organizations exist to make things better for those who we serve. We need to make it abundantly clear that we understand the pain and are uniquely qualified to address that pain. As we consider how to define our own superpowers, we need to keep that pain front and center.

So, now comes the time to identify your own organization's superpowers—the key areas where your organization can meet the needs of your customer family in a way that your competitors are not. There is no single ideal way to do this. Some will prefer a more organic approach. Some will prefer a more ordered approach. However you choose to approach it, you will be taking these three steps:

1. Identify potential superpowers by first aligning your organization's strengths with your customers' needs.
2. Narrow down your potential superpowers by aligning the strengths of your competitors against your potential superpower findings from the previous step.
3. Determine your ideal superpower and rephrase it in the form of a brief statement.

My recommendation for identifying areas of overlap is to start with your findings from just two of the constellations: the customer family, and your organization. I do this for two reasons. First, if you try to array all three constellations at once, you can end up having to sort through way too many options, some of which just won't really make sense. For example, your organization may have strengths that just don't align with the needs of your customer family. It's great to have strengths but the primary goal here is to uncover the strengths that matter most to your potential customers.

Starting your process by looking just at yourself and your customer also allows you to focus on that most important of relationships. After you have identified a few promising overlaps, then we will look at how our league of competitors informs where we want to place our ultimate focus.

One way to manage this is to create a table allowing you to see and evaluate all the possible combinations:

*Discover Your Organization's Superpower*

1. What are your organization's unique and legitimate strengths? As you are likely to have fewer distinguishing strengths than your customers have needs, distribute these in columns.
2. What are your customer family's unique needs? Distribute these in the rows.

Note, too, what you place in the rows at this point will limit your opportunities for potential superpowers. I can't stress enough that you should spend as much time as possible considering what your customer family's needs really are. If you leave anything off at this stage, you may lose the chance to consider it later. Be very thorough here. I also recommend you rank those needs in order to get a more structured analysis. Place the customers' top needs toward the top of the table.

As an example, let's look at a company offering HR management platforms. In the columns, we arrange three organizational strengths that we have identified: Top Customer Service Ratings, Full-Service Web-Based Platform, and Innovative Start-Up Company. In the rows we list a number of key findings from our customer research. Within the open cells, we indicate the areas where there is potential positive alignment between what our organization offers and what our customers need.

|  | **Your Organization's Strengths** |  |  |
| --- | --- | --- | --- |
| **Key Customer Traits (ranked)** | Top Customer Service Ratings | Full-Service Web-Based Platform | Innovative Start-Up Company |
| Preference for all-in-one solutions | Aligned | Aligned | Aligned |
| Strong need for short-term contracts | Aligned | No | Aligned |

|  |  |  |  |
|---|---|---|---|
| Tight budgets are the norm | Aligned | No | Aligned |
| Staff turnover is high | Aligned | Aligned | No |
| Low average employee salaries | No | No | No |
| Average company age under 10 years | No | No | Aligned |

We are attempting to rule out the combinations that just don't align, while bringing into focus the combination or combinations that do work. After you have identified the areas where your organization connects most meaningfully with your customers, you will bring your competitors into the analysis.

Perform this next step by creating several copies of the spreadsheet from the previous step. You can use one spreadsheet for each one of the key competitors in your league of competitors. The goal of this step is to gain a clear understanding of how your competitors themselves are aligned when it comes to the potential superpowers you defined in the previous step. I use a red, yellow, and green highlighting process to show if a competitor aligns itself with any specific attribute.

For example, in the prior step, we identified that our organization was aligned with the customer's "strong need for short-term contracts." In our second step, we color code the "strong need for short-term contracts" cell red if the competitor also uses this as one of its superpowers. We color code it green if the competitor does not use this attribute as a superpower. We color it yellow if it's somewhere between red and green.

When we are finished with the process, we will have one separate spreadsheet for each one of our key competitors. Each spreadsheet will have a number of color-coded cells. We are looking to see whether any of the particular cells are mostly green or yellow on all of the spreadsheets—indicating possible candidates for our superpower. We are also looking for cells colored mostly red when looking at all our competitors—indicating a superpower we may not be able to feature for our own organization.

After completing the first two steps, you should have a reasonably short list of those attributes that seem like the most promising candidates for your superpower(s). The next step will be to phrase each potential superpower in the form of a brief statement.

## Describing Your Organization's Superpower

Once you have completed the process of identifying your superpower candidates, it is very important to reframe them in the form of a brief statement. Doing so helps you to see the superpower in context—and context is what the DEEP process is all about.

> Begin to outline your statement as follows:
>
>> People are suffering because an important need isn't being met very well. Our organization meets this need exceptionally well, and in a way no one else does.
>
> For example:
>
>> Vegans don't want meat substitutes full of mega-processed ingredients. Our meat substitute is made from the natural ingredients you can find in your fridge. We even show you how we make it in our kitchens so you can make it in yours if you have the time.
>>
>> Working adults who return to school in order to complete a degree are, on average, saddled with $30,000 of debt—whether they finish their degrees or not. We assign each one of our students a personal financial counselor to ensure our graduates average under $10,000 of student debt.
>>
>> Most Americans report that visiting a new car dealership is more stressful than visiting a dentist. So, we don't even have a dealership. We bring two cars directly to your home so you can test drive and compare them both, on your own time, and where you won't feel any pressure at all.

A brief statement as seen in the examples above will serve as the jumping off point for the remaining phases of DEEP Marketing. Notice there is a lot of information embedded in each of the phrases. You can clearly identify a customer pain point and you can see the value your organization provides as a remedy to the pain point. Also embedded is the extensive research you have conducted in order to ensure that the statement captures the essence of what your organization does best, given the particular complexities of your competitive environment.

As we have seen, the first phase of DEEP Marketing is an exercise in getting very big in your thinking in order to condense things down to a simple and powerful statement of truth unique to your organization. In summary, the Discover phase is where we pin down the unique intersection(s) where we can:

- Apply our organization's unique strengths
- In order to solve a defined customer problem
- In a space that is competitively advantageous

*Figure 4*

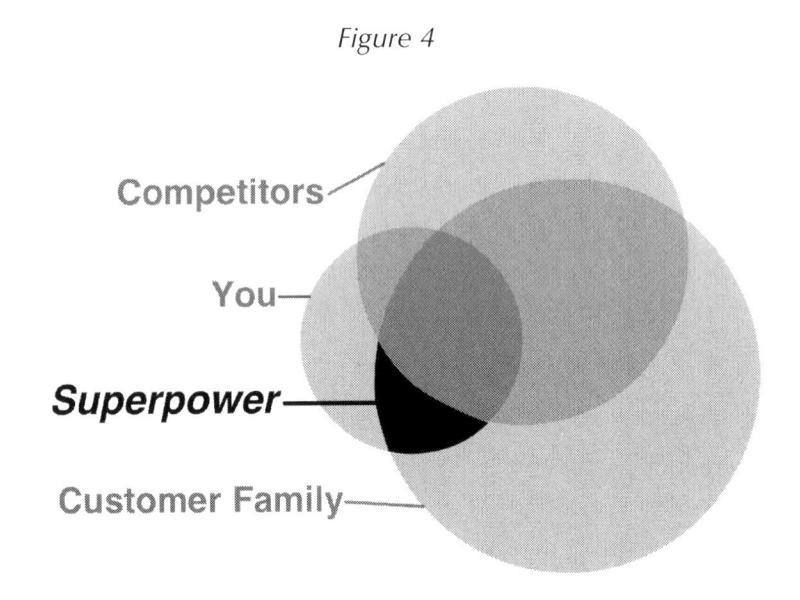

## Discover Your Organization's Superpower

As shown in Figure 4, the area labeled "Superpower" represents the desirable area where your organization can meet the needs of your customer family in a space where your competitors are not doing so.

In the next chapter, we will turn to the second phase in the DEEP Marketing process, which is designed to shape the findings from the Discover phase and give them structure. While it may seem our work is already complete, don't be tempted to move directly into external promotion—yet.

A lot of vitally important internal work remains to be done before we will be ready to project our findings out into the world.

CHAPTER 9

# Elaborate

THIS SECOND PHASE of the DEEP Marketing process is critically important because it is where we begin constructing the bridge that will span the gulf separating marketers from non-marketers in organizations. If the Discover phase seems familiar in terms of how organizations conduct their competitive analyses, then the *Elaborate* phase will likely seem unfamiliar.

The reason the first phase may seem familiar is because most organizations undertake some form of competitive analysis. Many, of course, go to great lengths. The problem is that these analyses nearly always reside within the marketing group's domain. It's important work, to be sure. But, again, the purpose of the DEEP Marketing model is to connect marketing and the marketing team with the rest of the organization.

In order to properly connect the first phase with the second, it is essential that the first phase be done as prescribed in Chapters 5 through 8. If we simply rely on mechanisms such as SWOT and PEST analyses, we are far less likely to be able to transition into the second phase successfully. Here's why.

SWOT or PEST analyses are probably the most common forms of competitive analysis used in organizations today. If your organization has undertaken one or both, then you likely ended up with some lengthy lists of key attributes. It is also likely that your findings weren't revelatory. Further, the attributes listed may not have been entirely accurate nor candid. It's just too easy to do a SWOT analysis poorly.

A common error with SWOT analyses occurs when the resulting lists of strengths and weaknesses share many of the same attributes: for example, listing "quick to innovate" as a strength while listing "too quick to innovate" as a weakness. If your organization can't determine whether a certain attribute is a weakness or a strength, then perhaps it is neither. Or, at least, the attribute is not being described clearly enough. I have also seen SWOT analyses where the results are simply bent to fit the direction the organization's leaders were aiming to go anyway.

The processes employed in the Discover phase must be taken seriously and approached with an open mind. You may end up turning your organization in a slightly new direction—its best direction. If an organization approaches the Discover phase openly and honestly, then this second step's purpose is to pressure test the findings. The phase is called "Elaborate" because its purpose is to demonstrate that our discovery from phase one can indeed serve as a meaningful and robust foundation for our external marketing.

If you consider the DEEP process to be parallel to the growth of a plant, then the Discover phase is where we create a seed. Seeds, if you aren't already aware, are amazing things. They are tiny (usually), they are durable, and they contain everything needed to launch a plant's growth once the seed is provided with water, heat and sunlight. The Elaborate phase is when the seed begins to grow its own roots. The Embrace phase is where the plant grows above ground and takes shape. And the Project phase is when the plant finally bears flowers and fruit.

## How to Conduct the Elaborate Phase

Similar to the way we get a seed to germinate, what we need to do now is prepare the soil and planting conditions in order to ensure that the seed can grow into a healthy plant. While an organization's marketing team drives the DEEP process, by definition it must be a very inclusive process. A seed needs a number of external elements and it is useful to think of the rest of the organization as providing those conditions for growth. The whole organization is essential if we want the seed to develop and eventually bear fruit.

Let's look at an example. Let's say your university has completed the Discover phase and your result was:

*Elaborate*

> Working adults who return to school in order to complete a degree are, on average, saddled with $30,000 of debt—whether they finish their degrees or not. We assign each one of our students a personal financial counselor to ensure our graduates average under $10,000 of student debt.

Preparing for success in this example means meeting with other members of your organization to discuss with them how they would help ensure that its graduates average under $10,000 of student debt. We must seek and employ the input of others within our organization since DEEP Marketing is an internal exercise as much as it is an external one.

Now, the budget ramifications of trying to establish and manage a $10,000 debt ceiling may very well cause your CFO to protest. After all, student-debt-based revenue is (regrettably) the very lifeblood of many universities. The need at this stage is to seek the CFO's expertise in imagining how a $10,000 debt ceiling could be made to work. Are there other financial instruments or partnerships that could be employed? Could a creative tuition pricing plan help ensure sufficient revenue? Could revenues increase under the plan? All of these questions and many more need to be explored at this point.

In addition, you'll meet with the head of financial aid to see how they could support an institutional directive that average student debt is kept below $10,000. You'll certainly want to meet with your advising team to get their input regarding how this could appeal to prospective students. How would it appeal to current students? Student services will be eager to weigh in on the plan, as well.

Now, these discussions aren't meant to be exhaustive. Getting everyone in the organization on board will come in the third phase. For now, we are pressure testing our discovery. Have we missed identifying any potential blockages? Are there any insurmountable legal or regulatory concerns? We need to uncover these issues before we get any further down the road.

In addition, these exploratory conversations will slowly begin to convince an ever increasing number of colleagues to support our discovery within the organization. This is an important step considering that individuals who don't lend their support can potentially impede success down the road.

Lastly, it is crucial that the organization's CEO is fully invested in the DEEP process at this time and no later. While marketing will continue to work away on developing the full process, the CEO must help build support.

Here's why.

Earlier, I alluded to a potential conversation with the university CFO regarding a $10,000 debt ceiling for students. Imagine such a conversation happening between the CFO and the chief marketing office (CMO). I don't think the conversation would go very far. The most likely way to persuade the CFO to participate is if the question comes from the CEO. The best way (and perhaps the only way) to get that CFO to fully engage in the effort is to have it come as an assignment from the CEO.

A compelling example of how this phase of DEEP Marketing can work is by considering the story of Henry Ford. In the first few years of the 1900s, Ford realized that if he could build a car and sell it for $500, there would be a massive market for his product. That was Ford's Discovery, and that's where his process began. However, at the time, cars were quite expensive to build and the idea that one could be built and sold—at a profit—for $500 would have been considered impossible by nearly anybody.

From Ford's autobiography:

> I will build a motor car for the great multitude... constructed of the best materials, by the best men to be hired, after the simplest designs that modern engineering can devise ... so low in price that no man making a good salary will be unable to own one—and enjoy with his family the blessing of hours of pleasure in God's great open spaces.[14]

Once Ford had articulated the vision, his next step was to elaborate the discovery. In other words, he had to shape his entire company around his vi-

---

[14] The Henry Ford. (n.d.). *Henry Ford Quotations*. Retrieved, July 1, 2021, from https://www.thehenryford.org/collections-and-research/digital-resources/popular-topics/henry-ford-quotes/

*Elaborate*

sion of a great and unprecedentedly affordable car. Ford and his team had to reimagine the automotive assembly line in order to see his dream come true. Ford didn't ask his team if they *could* build a great car for so little. They were asked *how* it could be done. Were it not for the founder's bold vision and his drive to see it though, the Ford Motor Company never would have obtained such massive success. By 1924, it is said that more than half of the cars in the world were Fords.[15]

It took a clear vision and it took persistence to make the mass-produced automobile a reality. But the vision came first.

If Ford had started by asking if his vision were possible, he would have met mountains of resistance. Instead, he led with a vision and willed it into reality. We can't all revolutionize our industries but if we have a singular vision and we push boundaries, we can be remarkably successful in serving our market.

Be aware that the worst case scenario in the Elaborate phase would be that, for some reason (or reasons), the organization finds it simply cannot operate successfully under the recently Discovered marketing statement. If that turns out to be the case—though it would be unlikely given the rigor of the first phase—then the marketing team would return to phase one and identify an alternative potential superpower to pressure test.

If the first seed just won't germinate, and if we absolutely can't alter the seed's growing conditions, then we must try with a new seed. Such is life.

Following is a list of the potential impacts you will want to assess during the Elaborate phase:

---

[15] Brinkley, D. (2003). *Wheels for the world: Henry Ford, his company, and a century of progress, 1903–2003*. Viking.

| Business Unit | Questions to Pressure Test |
|---|---|
| Finance | • What are the potential impacts on expenses?<br>• What are the potential impacts on revenues? |
| Legal/Regulatory | • Are there any legal concerns regarding the new Discovery?<br>• Are there any regulatory concerns regarding the new Discovery? |
| Human Resources | • What impacts will the new Discovery have on our human resources?<br>• Will we need to make any adjustments to staffing? |
| Technology | • What are the technology impacts for the new Discovery?<br>• Will it require new business intelligence capabilities? |
| Product/Service | • How would the Discovery reshape our product portfolio?<br>• Are certain products incompatible with the Discovery?<br>• How does the Discovery impact our product development process? |

These questions may seem a bit daunting in that they could give the appearance we are preparing to change everything about the organization and its processes. However, while your Discovery may appear somewhat jarring, it simply provides a more refined view of what you are already doing. The Discovery simply adds contextual clarity to what your organization does. The Discovery connects what you do well, with the things your customer family needs, and in a way that's highly aware of your competitors.

*Elaborate*

The Elaborate process is designed to help the entire organization get more closely in touch with what it already excels at naturally.

As stated before, at this point in the process we are beginning to build the superstructure supporting the well-grounded external communication that will come later. I use the term superstructure because we are building a bridge, after all. If you've ever seen a photo of a suspension bridge undergoing construction, you'll understand what I'm driving at.

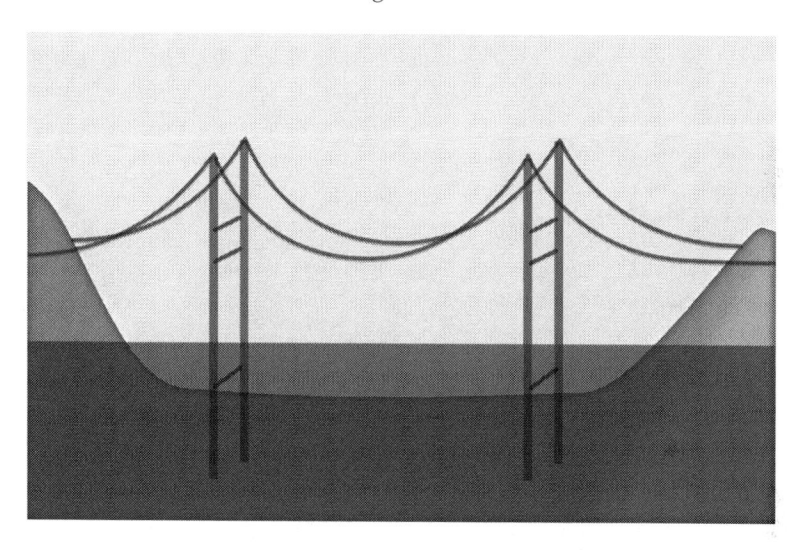

*Figure 5*

Built nearly 100 years ago, the Golden Gate Bridge today is a symbol of San Francisco and even of the state of California. The iconic bridge carries about 110,000 vehicles every day across the mile-wide mouth of the San Francisco Bay.[16] Although its construction was a feat of engineering and human labor, the bridge has a remarkably simple design (see Figure 5). Two tall pillars are embedded in the seafloor rising 750 feet above the water. From the tops of the pillars are draped two long cables that each stretch across the water to anchors on both shores. The bridge deck is then suspended from the

---

[16] Golden Gate Bridge Highway & Transportation District. (n.d.) *Annual Vehicle Crossings and Toll Revenues*. Retrieved July 1, 2021, from https://www.goldengate.org/bridge/history-research/statistics-data/annual-vehicle-crossings-toll-revenues/

*DEEP Marketing*

long cables. In other words, the core structure of the Golden Gate Bridge consists of two tall towers and two cables. That's it. The actual roadway hangs from the two cables.

During the Elaborate phase of DEEP Marketing, an organization figuratively builds the towers and cables supporting the new bridge that will connect its marketers and non-marketers. After these main components are built, we can hang all kinds of things from our bridge. We can paint it whatever color we want. We are open to many possibilities. But the core structure is what defines everything else.

In fact, in the Elaborate phase, we are developing what I call *Pillars*. Pillars are the two or three main concepts defining how our organization does what it does. Let's use the examples from Chapter 8. Here are three hypothetical superpowers that emerged from the Discover phase.

**Organization 1:**
Vegans don't want meat substitutes full of mega-processed ingredients. Our meat substitute is made from the natural ingredients you can find in your fridge. We even show you how we make it in our kitchens so you can make it in yours if you have the time.

**Organization 2:**
Working adults who return to school in order to complete a degree are, on average, saddled with $30,000 of debt—whether they finish their degrees or not. We assign each one of our students a personal financial counselor to ensure our graduates average under $10,000 of student debt.

**Organization 3:**
Most Americans report that visiting a new car dealership is more stressful than visiting a dentist. So, we don't even have a dealership. We bring two cars directly to your home so you can test drive and compare them both, on your own time, and where you won't feel any pressure at all.

The superpowers above each describe a problem and what the organization does to address the problem. In the first example, we have an organization that markets a meat substitute made from natural, everyday ingredients. Our Pillars need to tie into the superpowers in a way describing how we do

*Elaborate*

what we do. There are many ways an organization can market a meat substitute with natural ingredients but how does your organization do that?

First, I want to be more specific regarding what is meant by "how." How describes the manner in which your organization goes about its work. Hows are akin to personality traits. Does your organization emphasize technology? Does it emphasize doing things by hand? Does your organization approach things in a high energy manner or a more laid back manner? The examples in the following table will help:

|  | \multicolumn{3}{c}{"What" the Organization Does} |||
| --- | --- | --- | --- |
|  | **Meat substitutes made from ingredients you'd find in your fridge** | **A university where students graduate with minimal debt** | **New cars delivered to your driveway and no aggressive salespeople** |
| **"How" the Organization Does What it Does** | Product delivered to your door or via regular grocery channels? | High tech classrooms or low-budget approach? | Personal human concierge or virtual assistant? |
|  | Everything done to minimize products' footprint? | Offering business degrees only, or many majors? | Offering only inexpensive car models or including luxury brands? |
|  | Flash frozen or only fresh ingredients? | Online only or in-person teaching? | Offering full range of financing options? |

The research you performed in the Discover phase should help you a lot here. This is because how you do what you do must resonate with your customer family. Let's look at our meat substitute example again. Let's say in your research you learned that people who consume meat substitutes also shop at farmers markets much more than the average household. If that's the case, then you may wish to emphasize the fact that your organization works with farmers' cooperatives to source its ingredients. One of your Pillars might be "Food from Local Farming Communities."

You may also have learned in your research that concern for the environment is a characteristic running strong among your customer family. If so, then you might choose to include a second Pillar of "Food Products that Actually Improve the Environment."

The primary value of the Pillars is that an organization needs a few central characteristics about which it can repeatedly communicate, thereby helping to cement its unique appeal to consumers. People are more likely to become customers and stay customers if they are aligned with an organization's manner of doing business. In Chapters 11 and 12 we will learn more about how the Pillars are to be used.

CHAPTER 10

# Embrace

RECALL THAT THE overarching need for the DEEP Marketing model is to drive marketing deeper into the organization's core in order to connect the organization's externally facing marketing activities with all of its related internal activities. In the *Embrace* phase of DEEP Marketing, we train our focus upon getting the entire organization to embrace our findings from Phases 1 and 2.

For those who may suspect this sounds like an exercise in manufacturing buy-in, let me describe how the process avoids becoming contrived. To me, earning true buy-in means presenting a case so compelling that everyone in the organization will happily and spontaneously embrace it. If you do your work very well in the first two phases, then this third phase won't have that dreaded feel of a too-slick presentation from a branding agency. It will feel like an affirmation of purpose. And it should even feel exhilarating.

However, note that we aren't simply asking the rest of the organization to understand, weigh in on, or carry out what we learned in the Discover and Elaborate phases.

We are inviting the entire organization to realize and take ownership in the fact that they are all on the *marketing team*. We are asking everyone to contribute in their own special ways to make our organization's foundation even more solid.

This phase can be very exciting. In fact, it should be exciting for several reasons:

- Your work from the prior two phases provides you with a solid framework to share with staff.

- The framework has already absorbed the input and secured the approval from key individuals in the organization.
- The framework is not just coming from the marketing department or from an outside consultant.
- The process truly values everyone's input and participation.

Now, that last point may seem like asking a bit much for many organizations. After all, not all organizations are entirely populated by an engaged and upbeat staff. It's true many organizations have allowed too much cynicism to fester within their walls. Maybe for some organizations, this aspect of DEEP Marketing will appear to be impossible.

But I think you'll find that while you are likely to encounter some degree of pushback or cynicism at this phase, the vast majority of your employees will come along more than happily. If the Embrace phase doesn't progress in a fairly smooth manner right from the beginning, then either the prior work wasn't executed well (and you should fix it), or you may have some underlying HR issues needing to be dealt with.

## How to Conduct the Embrace Phase

The Embrace phase is the third phase in a four-part process. In the Discover phase, we created a seed. In the Elaborate phase we planted our seed within our organization and encouraged it to grow roots. In this third phase we will focus on encouraging healthy growth in the plant's branches and leaves before we move to the fourth phase when we will finally get to focus on the fruit and flowers—literally the messages our customers will see and, if all goes according to plan, respond to positively.

We learned in Chapter 1 that a lack of clarity among staff regarding external messaging is one of the key symptoms of dysfunction in marketing. That lack of clarity represents a steady stream of missed opportunities for free and highly valuable word-of-mouth marketing. One of the key purposes of this third phase, therefore, is to get everyone in the organization clear and aligned with one another regarding the organization's superpower or big idea.

*Embrace*

So, how do we go about creating that alignment? If we look at the ways organizations endeavor to build team spirit and consensus among staff, we typically see them bring in consultants to run workshops or lead team-building activities.

If you can, do a quick online search for "corporate team building" and see what you get. Your quick search should yield lots of paid and organic listings for companies offering team building activities and exercises. When I searched in late 2020, here's a sampling of what I saw:

- Book your team to drive a Porsche for the day
- Corporate boat memberships
- Escape From Hotel California
- Salsa Showdown
- Build Your Own Mini Golf Course
- 13 "Cool" team building exercises
- No trust falls. No blindfolds. Just the most FUN you'll ever have at work.

I'm sure many of these activities are truly a lot of fun. Sign me up. But notice two things. First, they are all based on playing games or having fun. Second, the focus of the team building exercises is to develop better communication, trust, and openness among team members. These are all good things to work on improving. So no issues there.

What's absent, though, is a purpose. The Embrace phase of DEEP Marketing has a very specific focus. The goal is to get everyone in the organization aligned with what we found in the first two steps. This is a critically important distinction. We aren't aimed at getting people to trust one another or to communicate better. We are cultivating internal alignment on what makes our organization matter. Consider some of the many benefits of having your staff aligned:

- Everyone in the organization will be able to share your brand message, and do it well. Your organization will thereby gain tens or hundreds or thousands of marketers to amplify the effectiveness of your current team of professional marketers.
- Your IT director can begin looking for ways to make your superpower come to life on internal and external software platforms.
- Your HR director will want to make your organization's superpower an important component in their new employee orientation programming.
- Your logistics department will be charged to find ways to marry their processes with the newly clarified superpower.
- Your facilities department can apply the superpower to inform selections of interior furnishings.

Chapters 11 and 12 will describe these benefits in greater detail. But now that we understand the key benefits, here are the steps for carrying out the Embrace phase of DEEP Marketing.

First, your marketing department will need to craft a 30–60-minute presentation designed to share its findings from Phases 1 and 2. The presentation will describe how you used the DEEP Marketing process to "fix" or perhaps "recalibrate" your organization's marketing. Now, this can be a bit sticky in that the goal isn't to throw marketing under the bus. The goal is simply to show that the organization's leaders realized there was an opportunity to take its marketing to a higher level.

The basic outline for your presentation should be as follows:

1. Marketing has identified a problem. Note: for your particular organization, the problem could be that its messaging needed to be tightened up in order to compete more effectively. Perhaps your problem is that there has been too much turnover in marketing. In any case, your presentation should start with an admission of a relatable problem. Many or even most individuals in the organization

*Embrace*

will be happy to hear marketing is being proactive and participating in an important process of improvement or reinvention.
2. The CEO has asked marketing to perform a thorough analysis of the situation and make recommendations.
3. Marketing has performed a thorough analysis of its customers, its competitors and of itself in order to identify key areas of opportunity.
4. The analysis uncovered key findings about its customers, its competitors and itself. Briefly describe the findings.
5. The nexus where these findings converge advantageously describes our organization's special place in the market. It is our organization's superpower.
6. We have already shared these findings with the CEO and several other key players. Our CEO is 100 percent on board.
7. We are now sharing our findings with you and the entire staff in small groups in order to hear and possibly incorporate your feedback and ideas before we begin to introduce the concept to those outside of our organization.
8. Ask for reactions and feedback. Listen and take notes.

Your S*uperpower presentation* should be arranged so that it is easy for non-marketers to understand. In other words, don't use marketing jargon. Keep the language straightforward and respectful. Finally, ensure the person or people leading the presentation know the material inside and out.

Once you've developed a draft presentation you are satisfied with, your following step will be to share the presentation in person with your entire marketing team. Set up a meeting and run through the presentation as if it were a dress rehearsal. Sharing in this way with the marketing team serves two purposes. It allows your marketing team to provide further refinements—which will make your presentation even better. It also provides an opportunity for the presenter to receive feedback on their delivery. Make sure to allow plenty of time at the end of the presentation for discussion.

After sharing with the marketing team and incorporating their suggestions for improvement, you will share the presentation with the organization's leadership team. Although this will feel like the most high-stakes step in the Embrace phase, you already will have secured your CEO's full buy-in. Make sure the CEO introduces the meeting with their clear and enthusiastic support. As mentioned earlier, the CEO's support is a requirement for this process. If the CEO is not 100 percent on board, then you are not ready to take this important step. Listen to feedback from the leadership team and, where possible, find ways to incorporate their input if doing so makes good sense.

After sharing the presentation with the leadership team, you will share the presentation with every department in your organization starting, in general, with those teams having the greatest volume of customer contact. This part of the process is not just important. It's necessary that you share the presentation with everyone. This is because one of the fundamental purposes of DEEP Marketing is to actually get people aligned. You can't achieve that by taking half-steps. You can only accomplish it by spending time face-to-face with the entire organization (or as much as is humanly possible if your organization is exceedingly large).

I have found that this step generates a lot of goodwill. The IT team, for example, usually doesn't get to hear a marketing presentation openly asking for and listening to their input. The same is true for the business office. You are likely to receive lots of thanks from your colleagues for making the important effort, which can help to make this step quite satisfying. But more importantly, this step gets you so much closer to finally fixing the problems that have been plaguing your marketing.

Only after you have shared your findings with the entire staff, and only after you've processed any valid input, will you be ready to polish your presentation one final time and prepare to share your new superpower with the outside world. The following chapters take a look at how we do that.

To summarize, the Embrace phase requires you to:

*Embrace*

1. Develop a presentation describing the prior steps you took as part of the DEEP process
2. Share the presentation with your marketing team
3. Share the presentation with your leadership team
4. Share the presentation with everyone else in your organization

Lastly, be aware that the Embrace phase needs to be treated as a living thing. It's not a one-and-done exercise for two reasons. First, new people will join your organization. New staff must be exposed to your Superpower presentation in some form as they join your organization. Secondly, staff who have already seen the presentation will need occasional reminders. Fortunately, reminders are less time-consuming than introductions. In addition, reminders can be fun. They can come in the form of short presentations at staff meetings. Reminders can show up in internal communications tools. The main idea is that a routine stream of reminders will serve to cement the superpower findings throughout the staff until they become hard-wired.

♦ ♦ ♦ ♦

After you have brought everyone in your organization on board, you will begin shifting your focus toward DEEP Marketing's final phase, which will be external facing. But before delving into the final phase, we need to condense and repackage our findings from the first three phases. Consider that those first three phases are quite dense. We gathered a tremendous amount of information, processed the information and boiled it down into an hour-long presentation. We need something even more concise to help inform all the external facing work we will be preparing in the last phase.

We achieve this by distilling our findings into one brief document called a *DEEP Connector.*

CHAPTER 11

# Your DEEP Connector

AS I WAS developing the DEEP Marketing framework, I realized that it aligned quite nicely with the iceberg metaphor. When the two concepts are combined (see Figure 6), it is easy to see there is much more to marketing than meets the eye.

*Figure 6*

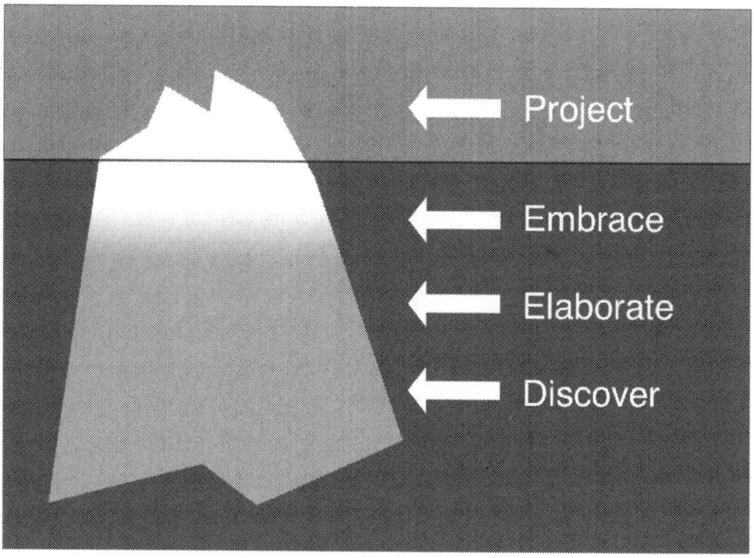

The first three steps in creating a successful marketing program (Discover, Elaborate, Embrace) occur below the waterline. Those three steps are completed within the organization and they involve the entire organization—not just the marketing staff. The steps are not in public view, but they provide the all-important foundation for what will eventually be built above the surface in public view.

Completion of the first three steps in the DEEP model will prepare you to construct what I call a DEEP Connector—a concise document that neatly sets forth your organization's marketing essence. The DEEP Connector is something that everyone in your organization should get to know very well. It is essentially a one-page overview of the presentation you developed and refined in the Embrace phase.

Here are the defining elements of your DEEP Connector:

- Your DEEP Connector should be referenced to help provide direction when making any important decisions for your organization.
- Your DEEP Connector doesn't expire when your current marketing leader leaves. It is specifically designed to survive after your current marketing leader exits and your new one arrives.
- Your DEEP Connector should last several years and will only have to change significantly when important elements in Phase 1 (Discover) force you to adapt.
- Your DEEP Connector must be brief if it's to be used and be effective. One page, one side … that's it.
- Your DEEP Connector should contain four elements: What, How, Why and the Narrative. In general, the fewer words, the better.
- There are many ways to format your own DEEP Connector, but brevity and clarity are key.
- Your DEEP Connector will contain the seeds of all your external communication, so it needs to be constructed with great care.

Let's take a closer look (see Figure 7).

*Figure 7*

## DEEP Connector Template

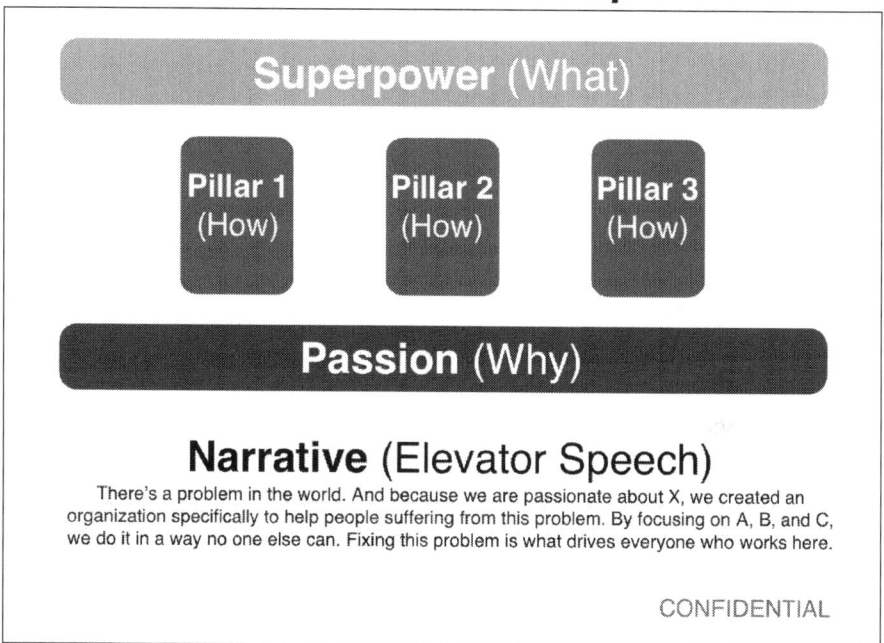

**Superpower** (What)

**Pillar 1** (How)   **Pillar 2** (How)   **Pillar 3** (How)

**Passion** (Why)

**Narrative** (Elevator Speech)

There's a problem in the world. And because we are passionate about X, we created an organization specifically to help people suffering from this problem. By focusing on A, B, and C, we do it in a way no one else can. Fixing this problem is what drives everyone who works here.

CONFIDENTIAL

First of all, the document is arranged in terms of message complexity. Concepts are simple up top and they get more nuanced as you progress down the document. There is a very important reason for this. People are bombarded with ads and unsolicited communication all day, every day. It is nearly impossible to get your target market to really hear—let alone understand—your mission statement or your sales pitch. If the vast majority of your communication is delivered via short and punchy messages, however, you will vastly increase your odds of being remembered and nudging your prospective customer into the first phase of your conversion funnel (refer to Figure 2 in Chapter 1).

Put another way, you need to get your foot in the door in order to get your potential customer to eventually open it. And there's no better way to get one's foot in the door than with something small and concrete. Therefore, the top of the DEEP Connector represents *what* your organization is all about in its most stripped down form. If there were only one word (or a very short combination of words) that your organization could be synonymous with—that your organization could own—it would be this one word. This word is your mantra. Your North Star. It should be used more than any other word in your communications.

The next level down on your DEEP Connector shows the three main ways your organization works in order to accomplish that one core word. These are your Pillars and they describe *how* your organization does what it does. For those potential customers who have heard or been exposed to your core word enough times, your three Pillars will be the next thing to be heard and understood. As message volume accumulates, potential customers will start to form a fuller picture of what your organization does and how it does it. The messaging will serve to drive prospective customers closer still to engagement.

The third level down is an expression of your organization's passion. Recall from Chapter 7 our discussion about an organization's passion. Passion is deeper than purpose. Purpose is selling the freshest bread that money can buy. Passion is getting up at 4 a.m. every morning to bake because you love baking and sharing it with others. Passion describes *why* your organization even exists.

Finally, at the bottom of the document, is the *Narrative*. The narrative is a very brief paragraph consolidating everything neatly. The narrative will directly reference all three tiers of your DEEP Connector, but will do so in proper English. It serves as the script for your elevator speech.

Recall that your organization's staff can serve to amplify your marketing message if they are armed with an appropriate elevator speech. In order to be effective, the elevator speech must meet three conditions. It must be: (a) meaningful, (b) motivating, and (c) memorable. The DEEP Connector and the narrative section in particular are designed to meet each of these three conditions. In outline form, it should say:

> There's a problem in the world. And because we are passionate about X, we created an organization specifically to help people suffering from this problem. By focusing on A, B, and C, we do it in a way no one else can. Fixing this problem is what drives everyone who works here.

It's important for me to note here that the DEEP Connector appears to start with what, and then moves to how, and finally to why. In his groundbreaking TED talk (the third-most-watched TED talk of all time), the acclaimed marketing strategist Simon Sinek introduces an idea he calls, "Start with Why."[17] Sinek argues that organizations must lead with their why in order to connect more authentically with consumers. I am a fan of what Sinek says.

However, what we uncovered in Part 1 of this book is the tremendous dysfunction that exists in marketing in organizations today. In my experience, the risk in "starting with why" is that it can tend to make a very subtle and complex process sound far too simple, especially to non-marketers. Most organizations will have a hard enough time trying to articulate their "why," let alone find a way to embrace and activate their "why." On the other hand, DEEP Marketing and the DEEP Connector connect an organization's what, how and why into a single cohesive unit, which is a more holistic and practical model for organizations wishing to fix their marketing.

## What Your DEEP Connector is Not

Your DEEP Connector is not your mission or vision statement. The DEEP Connector is direct and action-inducing, unlike most organizations' vision statements or mission statements, which are better known for gathering dust and not stoking the emotions.

Your DEEP Connector is not an external document. It is intended for insiders and an organization's partners only. The document should always have "Confidential" printed or watermarked on it. If you were a coach, the DEEP Connector would be your list of plays. You don't want your opposing teams to see your playbook while you are planning to play against them.

---

[17] TED. (2019, September). *How great leaders inspire action*. [Video]. https://www.ted.com/talks/simon_sinek_how_great_leaders_inspire_action?language=en

They'll be able to tease out many of the details of your playbook after they've played you. So, view your DEEP Connector as an internal document you want to keep mostly under wraps.

## Why is it Called a DEEP Connector?

I've spent a lot of time considering and evaluating scores of potential names for this important document. So, I think it's important that I share why I ended up choosing "DEEP Connector."

The Deep Connector serves as a marketing and communications platform in that it forms the foundation from which an organization's external marketing should arise. However, I very intentionally did not want to label it a "marketing" document because doing so would signal that it is owned by the marketing department. And because there is such a dysfunctional understanding between marketers and non-marketers, it was important the document not be seen—and immediately brushed off—as a "marketing" doc.

It is essential that everyone in the organization feels pride of ownership in the document. The document belongs to the entire organization—not to marketing.

Further, the document is highly businesslike. It does not contain a lot of flowery language. It is hierarchically organized. In many ways, it's like a blueprint or a recipe in that it contains the basic elements and instructions that make your organization uniquely suited to what it does. The content of the document is a summation of the DEEP Marketing process.

Most importantly, though, the document is designed to facilitate connections. The document is intended to interconnect the activities of everyone within the organization. It connects those activities to a deeper purpose. And the document is meant to help connect the organization with its external partners and eventually to the world outside.

Therefore, the document is, more than anything, a connector. After all, the primary purpose of DEEP Marketing is to address the gaps in understanding that exist between marketers and non-marketers—gaps that are

*Your DEEP Connector*

causing great dysfunction for organizations. So, the one thing DEEP Marketing must do is to foster connections both within the organization, and between the organization and its market. If an organization can be seen as an iceberg, then the DEEP Connector is what binds the visible parts of the iceberg to the invisible parts below.

CHAPTER 12

# How Your DEEP Connector Will Help You

THE MAIN PURPOSE of the first three phases of the DEEP Marketing process is, again, to construct a solid and well-integrated foundation for our external communication. So, it is imperative that we build everything upon the bedrock of those first three phases accordingly. Naturally, this means the marketing team will use the findings from the first three phases to shape its communication strategies and tactics. But it also means we will need to prepare the non-marketers on how to use our discovery.

Recall that a key aspect of the disconnect between marketers and non-marketers is the lack of a shared messaging vocabulary. Once an organization has completed the first three phases of DEEP Marketing, it will have a DEEP Connector, and will thereby possess something as close to a shared vocabulary as is possible. The entire staff will all have access to and be using the same words in their communication. As such, every interaction anyone on the staff has with anyone outside of the organization will reinforce every other message.

Your DEEP Connector will help your organization tremendously—but only if you use it. And only if you use it the right way. This chapter will look at the many ways your DEEP Connector can help your organization. Before plunging in, I offer special guidance to the leaders of organizations.

## A Note for CEOs

DEEP Marketing is *your* tool.

The effectiveness of DEEP Marketing depends upon your commitment to follow the process through and it can't fix your organization's problems without your leadership. Too often organizations undertake initiatives for improvement without following through. In this important sense, DEEP Marketing is like any effort to make systemic improvement. Whether it's something you are doing to improve your health or to improve your business, you must first have a winning plan—and you must then follow the plan.

Recall that the problem we are trying to solve here is that there is a disconnect between the marketers and the non-marketers in your organization. The way to address the gap (as discussed in Chapter 9) is to build a bridge. The DEEP Marketing process yields a DEEP Connector, which will serve as your bridge. But a bridge can simply be a bridge to nowhere if you don't use it to connect the opposing sides. CEOs and their organization's top leaders must use the bridge.

More importantly though, the bridge will not be able to do its job if it is allowed to be torn down and rebuilt every year. If that is allowed, then you'll never really have a bridge. What you'll have instead is an endless construction project. With you, the CEO, taking the lead, and with the passage of a little time, the entire organization will fully appreciate the value of the bridge as an essential and iconic piece of your organization's infrastructure.

Think about some of history's more iconic marketing campaigns:

- "Just Do It" - Nike
- "Think Different" - Apple
- "The Ultimate Driving Machine" - BMW
- "A Diamond is Forever" - DeBeers (in use since 1947)
- "Can You Hear Me Now?" - Verizon
- "15 Minutes Could Save You 15 Percent or More on Car Insurance" - GEICO

All day long, organizations are asking their marketing teams to develop something that can deliver the same magic as these campaigns. They instruct their creative agencies to give them something as good. One of Verizon's competitors even uses the same actor in their attempt to repeat Verizon's suc-

## How Your DEEP Connector Will Help You

cess. Many of GEICO's competitors have adopted the same flavor of kitschy humor in their campaigns. But don't think that it's solely the brilliant idea that makes these campaigns great.

What makes the campaigns iconic isn't only that they came up with a solid idea. What enabled those great ideas to become iconic is that they stuck with the ideas.

The campaigns were given time to mature and grow. The campaigns lived sufficiently long to allow customers to become familiar with, and embrace their message. The campaigns' key feature is that they were given enough time to seep into the consciousness of the target audience. Sure, the organizations all spent incredible amounts of money in advertising—far more than many of our own organizations will ever spend on marketing. But as important as the money, they spent a lot of time.

So, even if your organization will never be able to spend a fortune on a great campaign, it can surely spend a lot of time with it.

Your DEEP Connector provides the superstructure from which your organization can build its own iconic campaign. As CEO, you must protect the DEEP Connector even as marketing leaders come and go. When GEICO brings in a new head of marketing, their first order of business isn't to completely change their winning formula. Their job is to refine the campaign, to extend it, to provide yet more opportunities for customers to engage and connect with it.

Your DEEP Connector will allow your marketing team to focus productively on execution rather than on reinventing the wheel every 12 months. Once your organization has undergone the DEEP Marketing process, your new CMO's job won't be building bridges, their job will be to make smart and steady improvements to a bridge that already exists.

Since DEEP Marketing involves an investment in time, fortunately there are ample ways to extract compounding returns upon that investment. Following are specific examples of how your organization can make the most of its new DEEP Connector.

## Using Your DEEP Connector With External Partners

We've spent a lot of time exploring how DEEP Marketing can build bridges within organizations. Nevertheless, marketing is eventually about connecting an organization with what's outside of the organization. Fortunately, one of the most powerful aspects of your DEEP Connector will be revealed when you share it with your partnering organizations.

Partners come in many shapes, including: advertising agencies, sponsors, media partners, digital agencies, banks, auditors, IT and HR vendors, accrediting bodies, and so on. Fortunately, your DEEP Connector is something you can share with these partners. All your partners will benefit from having a clearer understanding of how you define your role in the marketplace. That knowledge will help them tailor their services to you. In short, you'll get more from them without spending more.

Let's look at the following table to see how the DEEP Connector can be used for various types of partners.

| Partner Type | Uses for your DEEP Connector |
| --- | --- |
| Marketing Agencies | • Use when screening new agencies to gauge level of shared passion<br>• Use as preface for creative kick-off meetings<br>• Use when reviewing creative concepts<br>• Use when reviewing media plan proposals |
| Shareholders | • Use to inform and persuade existing and potential investors about your clarity of purpose<br>• Tie performance measurements back to DEEP Connector to demonstrate effective deployment of resources |
| Sponsors | • Use in sponsorship proposals in order to identify clearer alignment of purpose between your organization and sponsor<br>• Use in sponsorship wrap-up documents to validate performance |

*How Your DEEP Connector Will Help You*

| Accreditors | • Use to demonstrate clarity of purpose and adherence to core standards when applying for and renewing accreditations |
|---|---|
| Financial Partners | • Use when choosing banks and auditors to test for alignment in purpose, and willingness of the partner to provide a higher level of service and lower fees<br>• Use to demonstrate clarity of purpose and adherence to plans |
| Vendors | • Use when screening all potential vendors (software, hardware, furniture, HR outsourcing, parts suppliers, etc.) to assess shared opportunities and negotiate for more favorable terms |

As you can see, DEEP Marketing doesn't only address your own internal marketing problems. It also helps you leverage the strengths of your partnering organizations in order to generate additional value for your organization.

## Using Your DEEP Connector Internally

Investing in the bottom of your organization's "iceberg" strengthens the radiance of what's above the waterline.

Seen another way, deepening the marketing understanding within an organization is akin to a runner or golfer improving their performance by focusing on their core or their fundamentals, rather than by focusing on their shoes or their clubs. We hear so much about staying flexible and embracing all that's new in the world. But what matters more than flexibility is having a solid core from which to manage and direct flexibility. Elite athletes and coaches know this. Power comes from one's core. Agility and speed are critically important but the utmost expression of agility and speed requires a solid core.

For organizations, investing in your core means that your communication will be aligned to something powerful. Every external message you create will be supported by your DEEP Connector. Every sales pitch. Every customer service communication. The visuals you choose. The music you employ. Your published content. And so on. The point is that your stream of communication and your brand essence will become clearer and easier to understand to those outside your walls. And in our current sea of media, it's absolutely essential that your communication be structured in a way enabling it to become clear to your desired audience.

What, then, about your internal communications? Shouldn't your internal messages, too, be packed with meaning to keep your entire team on the same page with respect to the organization's passion and purpose? If one of the key symptoms of dysfunction in marketing is that employees aren't on the same page with respect to messaging, then the DEEP Connector must be used in order to erase the symptom.

Consider the employee lifecycle. For most employees, there is an application and interview process, then an onboarding process, then ongoing employment, including periodic review processes which could also include promotions, and finally separation of employment. Your DEEP Connector can be used to improve upon the employer-employee bond in each of these stages.

First, language reflecting your DEEP Connector should be included in your recruiting materials, ads and posts. Don't let your HR department simply include a job description along with their approved language. Augment their materials with language that was specifically developed to appeal powerfully with organizational outsiders. Make sure each one of your applicants knows what your organization is all about. Share with them your purpose. Doing so helps prospective employees understand so much more about your organization from their very first interaction with you. It will also heighten the motivation of those candidates who already feel a resonance with your message. In a perfect world, wouldn't you rather be screening candidates who share your organization's passion?

Continue in the interview process. Ask candidates to explain to you what they think your organization is about and why that excites them. Make sure each of your internal interview team members has a copy of your DEEP Connector in their interview materials for handy reference. This will plant

## How Your DEEP Connector Will Help You

the seed within your candidates that your organization's purpose is all-important. Let them know this right from the start.

Next, make sure to include a streamlined version of the DEEP Marketing Superpower presentation in the employee's orientation activities within their first few days. Don't simply rely on your organization's mission statement or vision to achieve this—those aren't written with the same purpose. Sharing the Superpower presentation immediately tells the employee what the organization is all about … what really matters.

New employees have a lot on their plates. There are onboarding activities, meetings with fellow staff members, and learning new systems. The term, "Drinking from the fire hose" is a very accurate descriptor for any employee's first months on the job. So, give those employees a strong, clear message or else you will lose an important, but fleeting, bonding opportunity.

Ongoing employees, too, need continual reminders of what your DEEP Connector is. Provide desk copies for everyone. Talk about aspects of the DEEP Connector in staff meetings. Make it part of your routine activities. Just as importantly, include it in your performance review processes. How does each individual support the spirit of the DEEP Connector? Provide opportunities for employees to express their support and elevate those who really exemplify the tenets of your DEEP Connector. That, too, will cement your DEEP Connector's central importance.

Your DEEP Connector can also be used to enhance workforce cohesion and effectiveness by influencing your organization's performance-monitoring systems.

Here's how.

We've all been there. The Monday morning weekly leadership team meeting or a quarterly board meeting, and we get to review our KPI dashboard to report how sales and marketing are performing. So we run through a series of dashboard metrics to demonstrate how our sales funnels are shaping up. How is web traffic? How are conversions? Which campaigns are performing well? We review CPCs (cost-per-click), CPLs (cost-per-lead), ROAS (return on ad spend). We do our best to encapsulate everything into a quick-view dashboard to help an audience of non-marketers evaluate marketing performance.

But do these dashboards truly help or are they giving us a fuzzy view? The over-rationalization of marketing, as I label it, describes the way leaders are increasingly focusing on tactical performance data without investing in or fully grasping the overarching strategic framework that should be driving the tactics.

Let's face it, how important are CPCs when your creative is indistinguishable from that of your competitors? How much should your board members care about driving down CPLs when your sales team isn't armed with language crafted specifically to deepen a prospective customer's desires?

Your dashboard may be telling the leadership "all is good." Numbers are trending in the right direction. But you may well have underlying problems that aren't being highlighted.

This happens all the time. We curate the data we wish to share. We highlight what we want the board to see. As expected, board members typically seem pleased to see a dashboard awash in green lights. But when the bottom line starts to suffer and all the green lights begin shifting toward the red, it's often accompanied by a sudden realization that it may be time to hire a new agency or even bring in a new marketing leader.

The root issue here is that we aren't configuring our dashboards to tell us all we really need to know. In my opinion, we have become pathologically reliant upon the KPIs our dashboards (PowerBI, Tableau, mobile apps, etc.) provide—even in our day-to-day lives.

For example, many of us pore over the newfound wealth of health data from our smart devices when we exercise. Now that we have access to the metrics, we are driven to improve our VO2 max, lower our resting heart rates and accumulate more steps each day. In doing so, we slowly lose touch with why we are exercising at all: which is to be more healthy, to live a longer and less troubling life, to have less pain, or maybe to win some competitions. These end goals are clearly more important than the assorted metrics on the dashboard.

*How Your DEEP Connector Will Help You*

These newly unearthed troves of health data were once available only to elite coaches and athletes. But now the data is available to amateurs who, by and large, lack the deep knowledge required to interpret and apply all the data that the dashboards are showing us. Similarly, when we are reporting marketing performance in our leadership meetings, our audience (for the most part) does not possess an equivalent depth of marketing expertise, so we simply share the data and use some green, yellow and red lights to indicate health.

Our organizations don't exist simply to generate leads and sales. They have a deep purpose. And this deep purpose needs to be highlighted alongside our more visible health indicators.

Think of it this way: Does our organization exist to move customers through our sales funnel quickly? Is our customer promise that, "We will get your business for as little ad spend as we possibly can"? Of course not. We are telling our customers that they will receive relief for a significant problem that they need us to help them solve. Our dashboards should therefore be recalibrated to tell us how well we are achieving *that*.

If your university, as an example, says in its messaging that it's the best at getting recent graduates hired, then this is something you must be measuring and reporting on in every aspect of your organization. How are you ensuring post-grad hiring? How are you measuring it? What leading indicators exist? What are those indicators telling you? What's your financial aid department doing to help ensure post-grad hiring? What is your faculty doing to support hiring? Everyone needs to be engaged. And every department should have at least one dashboard metric tied to the organization's promise.

This reconfigured approach to KPIs provides a more meaningful health check while putting everyone on the same page with respect to what defines success. In doing so, marketing success becomes everyone's responsibility. And when your organization's marketing belongs to everyone, you should see your customer-oriented efficiencies improve across the board.

♦ ♦ ♦ ♦

Marketing frameworks are designed to help marketers optimize the external mechanisms that connect their organizations with their customers. What makes the DEEP Marketing framework unique is that it also focuses on the internal mechanisms that support—or in many cases sabotage—those externally facing mechanisms.

So, before we switch gears and start examining those all-important external connections in the next chapter, take a brief moment to remind yourself that the DEEP Connector is also a tool you should be using to strengthen your organization's internal connections.

# CHAPTER 13

# Project

FINALLY, WE GET to train our focus upon the many ways we project our marketing out into the world. Notice that it's not until this last phase that our marketing is deemed ready to travel beyond the walls of our organization. This final phase is when we unleash the power we have harnessed in the preceding phases. Notice, too, that this phase constitutes what most non-marketers incorrectly see as the entire scope of marketing.

The *Project* phase of DEEP Marketing is where the marketing, communications and sales teams get to open up and hit their stride. Surprisingly, the Project phase of DEEP Marketing is less prescriptive than the first three phases because this is the phase marketers already live and breathe. The phase involves marketing plans, creative development, marketing tactics, and all the things marketers already know how to do.

The key improvement your external marketing will enjoy with DEEP Marketing is that the marketing team will now be working from a foundation that is far more robust and solid, and which will resonate with, and be understood by, the entire organization. Recall that the primary purpose of DEEP Marketing is not to prescribe how to write or implement a marketing plan. Those are skills your marketing team should already have. The purpose of DEEP Marketing is to drive marketing deeper into the organization so that every ounce of the organization's external communication will be far more connected and effective.

Throughout the remainder of this chapter, then, we will look at how to apply DEEP Marketing to our organizations' external marketing activities: from developing a marketing plan to developing creative assets. In the following two chapters, we will examine the various marketing channels marketers use to communicate with potential and current customers. In order to make the most of DEEP Marketing, it's important to understand how each of the various channels works and it helps to understand how the channels are evolving.

## How to Conduct the Project Phase

As we have done every step along the way with DEEP Marketing, we will start at a more strategic level and work our way down to tactics, even in this last phase. So, let's look first at how to apply DEEP Marketing in our organization's marketing planning.

First of all, there is no one right way to craft a marketing plan. Marketing plans can be fairly brief or extremely long but nearly all start with some form of market overview. Fortunately, your extensive findings from the Discover phase of DEEP Marketing will make it relatively easy for you to develop your market overview. It's important, too, that your marketing plan reference the same three constellations we used in the Discover phase: (a) the customer family, (b) the league of competitors, and (c) the organization itself.

For example, if we originally included all universities in our analysis of our league of competitors, and then we later decided our true superpower didn't have any meaningful expression with relation to community colleges, we could eliminate them from consideration in our marketing plan. The idea here is to ensure that the market overview in your marketing plan focuses on your market as determined by your work in the first phase of DEEP Marketing.

Next, make sure the audience segmentation components of your marketing plan are informed by and align with your findings in the Discover phase. In conducting that phase you will have learned that your customer family possesses a number of uniquely defining traits and characteristics. The additional definition will help you and your media partners develop buyer personas, messaging, and media strategies that are more tightly focused on the audience segments you are trying to reach and persuade with your marketing.

As an example, let's say your organization sells healthy prepared foods and you have determined that a key market segment is single-income parents with two or more children living at home. In addition, perhaps your DEEP Con-

*Project*

nector features "Safety" as one of its Pillars. If this were the case, then you could layer "Safety" on top of your market segment, which could allow you to target a dimension your competitors may not be targeting. You could look at sponsoring events where families with young children get advice about children's car seats or bicycle helmets. In other words, the "Safety" component of your DEEP Connector allows you to interact with potential customers in environments less cluttered with competitors.

Once the marketing plan overview and segmentation are aligned with your findings in DEEP Marketing, you can begin to think about building out your multi-channel marketing tactics. Each channel will require creative assets and/or content. Whether in the form of video or audio (for online or offline channels), simple visual (for online, outdoor and print), or text only (search engine marketing), you will obviously want to ensure that every asset you create and send out into the world is crafted with a very high degree of purpose. So, before we look at each of these channels individually in the next chapters, let's look at the creative assets that will need to be created first.

## Creative Development

We all live in an environment that is overrun with media. In the pre-internet 1970s, it is estimated that Americans were exposed to between 500 and 1,600 ads per day. In 2021, the estimated exposure is 6,000 to 10,000 ads per day.[18] If you deduct eight hours for sleep, the average is 375 to 625 ads per hour, every hour of every day. No matter how you slice it, we are swimming in ads.

The ad environment is like a rainstorm. It's just coming down, so we keep on going but we duck our heads or hide under our umbrellas in order to get about our business. It's hard to notice any single particular raindrop. So, keep it in the very front of your mind that not only is your organization competing, your ads, too, are competing. Your ads are competing against your competitors' ads and competing against all other ads. Further, your competitors might be doing a really great job with their marketing. Your marketing

---

[18] Carr, S. (2021, February 15). *How Many Ads Do We See A Day In 2021?* PPC Protect. https://ppcprotect.com/how-many-ads-do-we-see-a-day/

doesn't operate in a direct line between you and your potential customer. There is a ton of interference between those two points. I can't stress how important it is that your creative executions are developed with this awareness front and center.

Say something striking, and then say it again and again.

Not only must your ads (and your content, your social posts, your website, your search results, etc.) stand out in some way, they also, of course, must be on message. So, even if your ads are consistent, and even if your ads are memorable, they still must communicate the message that you need them to communicate. To many, the advertising and communication process seems so straightforward—just put out some ads and start taking orders. But the process is remarkably complex.

Given the complexity, many organizations choose to work with agencies to help them with their creative development. In my opinion, using a creative agency is almost always a smart idea. There are three reasons for this. First, let's consider the risk.

Communication isn't precise. It's fuzzy. We work hard to craft messages that minimize the fuzziness but every dollar your organization spends on advertising media is, frankly, something of a calculated risk. So, in order to reduce the risk and the organization's financial exposure, we should hedge our investment by allocating an appropriate amount for creative development. The investment in creative development will reduce the downside risk of your more substantial media investment. It's just smart business sense.

The second reason to use a creative partner is that great creative ideas are more likely to come from people with special training and skills. Unless your organization can afford to pay dedicated staff to handle your creative needs exceptionally well, then contracting the skill makes financial sense.

The third reason for using a creative partner is that creative agencies do their best work when they have a client who provides direction. Consider that agencies are, more often than not, working for a stable of clients. Some of those clients will be directionless. Many, many are. Those clients leave all the

*Project*

work to the agency and frequently end up dissatisfied simply because they weren't able to compellingly articulate what they wanted in the first place. Such clients tell the agency that they just want their ads to "work" or that they want leads and or sales to increase—which puts far too much responsibility in the hands of the agency.

When you work with an agency after you've done the hard work of creating a DEEP Connector, you will find yourself with a happy and productive agency. Here's why.

Your DEEP Connector clearly lays out what your agency's work needs to accomplish. An important early mentor in my career is the co-founder of a major west coast advertising agency started in Seattle. He once confided in me, "Clients get the work they deserve." He explained that he simply meant clients can be their own biggest allies—or their own worst enemies—in the quest for great creative work. How right he was.

Organizations spend a lot of money on creative development and production. I've learned the hard way that the agency-client interface is one aspect of marketing that rarely gets managed well. Perhaps it is one of the reasons why your own marketing results aren't living up to their promise.

There are three main reasons creative breakdowns occur:

## Reason 1: Clients Come to the Table With Too Little Direction

Many clients look to agencies to do all the heavy lifting, which sort of makes sense since agencies are typically paid quite well. Furthermore, the process of selecting an agency can be tiring enough. However, the real work begins after the agency is chosen. And the first task is to provide a simple and specific set of expectations as to what the creative work needs to achieve. As the client, you should have a DEEP Connector in place describing your customers' needs, how your organization fills those needs, and how you are different from your competitors. It should also describe what you do, how you do it, and why you do it.

I have found that agencies are thrilled to have clear direction as it allows the first round of creative to be all the more on point.

## Reason 2: Creative Feedback Lacks Focus and Purpose

After you provide direction to the agency, they will then come back to you with a number of potential creative directions. At that point, it becomes your job to ask the agency to refine the work specifically in terms of how well it performs against what your DEEP Connector requires:

- Why are we using this tone?
- Why these colors?
- How does the messaging bring the DEEP Connector to life?
- Does it adequately capture the pain of your customers' problems?
- Is it conveying your unique ability to solve the problems?
- Does it look like your competitors' creative?
- How will the concept be applied across all channels?
- Does the concept provide opportunities to match the message with various media (for example, does the concept scream for outdoor)?
- Is that good or bad?
- How will it work on the many assorted social channels?

Ask the agency to elaborate upon these questions in order to get a full picture of how deep you can take the messaging. Remember, your goal is to get the most from your creative agency. Asking a lot of questions during this phase will refine the work … and make both you and your agency happier.

## Reason 3: Client Approvals Aren't Managed Correctly

After all the work and due diligence are complete, you'll need to secure final approvals from key members in your organization. This is the worst stage during which to have a creative breakdown, because a lot of billable hours will have been invested. But breakdowns happen here a lot. Often, a

*Project*

board member or CFO will want to weigh in at this late hour. But the arbiter of good creative isn't likely to be your CFO. What does your CFO know about marketing anyway? Do you ask your head of marketing about thorny accounting issues? Probably not. So, refrain from doing the opposite. If the CEO doesn't hold the line here, then results (and budgets) will almost certainly suffer.

What matters most is that the creative work maps directly to what your DEEP Connector requires. So, make sure your approval team only includes individuals who understand the DEEP Connector and who understand that their role is in ascertaining whether the work performs well against the DEEP Connector. Personal opinions and preferences regarding color schemes or humor or copywriting shouldn't dominate during this phase. Nor should the random opinions of individuals who are not marketing savvy. CMOs and CEOs need to select their list of approvers very judiciously. And someone must adequately brief the approvers on the DEEP Connector.

Handled correctly, final approvals will not be a time for ambushes.

Whether managing your creative work internally or working with an agency, your DEEP Connector will provide critically important structure allowing your organization to confidently sidestep the pitfalls likely to be encountered when producing ads and other creative assets.

CHAPTER 14

# Using DEEP Marketing in Paid Media Channels

NOW THAT WE have explored how DEEP Marketing will apply to your marketing planning and to your creative development, let's take a look at specific media channels and activities, starting with the channels consuming the most budget.

First, note there are many ways to categorize all the various marketing channels and the classification criteria are continually shifting as technologies evolve and merge. For our purposes here, marketing channels and activities are organized into three primary categories: paid, shared and owned. This chapter will focus on paid channels and the following chapter will focus on shared and owned channels.

As seen in the following table, paid media includes paid search engine marketing, paid online, paid social, and paid offline advertising. The category applies to any instance where your organization is paying to place an ad on a platform your organization doesn't own. There are a few gray areas, sponsored content for example, which I include in the category of shared media.

| Primary Category | Channel | Examples |
|---|---|---|
| **Paid Media**<br><br>Activities where your organization shares its message by directly paying another organization for access to its large audience. | Paid Search Engine Marketing (SEM) | Google, Bing, Yahoo, Baidu, etc. |
| | Paid Online Advertising | Usually handled by digital agencies using ad serving networks such as Google, Facebook, AdRoll, Amazon |
| | Paid Social Advertising | Paid placements on Facebook, Instagram, LinkedIn, etc. |
| | Paid Offline Advertising | TV, Radio, Outdoor, Print, Direct Mail |
| **Shared Media**<br><br>Activities where your organization shares its message by developing content for other organizations to share with audiences on their platforms. | Social Media and Content Marketing | Facebook, Instagram, Tik-Tok, sponsored content on news sites |
| | Earned Media | Media releases published on news or information sites. |
| | Experience Marketing | Events your organization sponsors |

## Using DEEP Marketing in Paid Media Channels

| | | |
|---|---|---|
| **Owned Media**  Marketing activities where your organization shares its message via channels it controls completely. | Web and Email | Your organization's own web properties, landing pages, blogs, email marketing |
| | Sales and Customer Service Language | Scripts and cues used by your staff who have direct customer contact |
| | Brand Assets | Your organization's logo, colors, voice, etc. |

Paid media is the category that gives rise to the most handwringing within organizations. The reason is not surprising. Money is involved—oftentimes large sums of money—and despite the significant investment, organizations often don't see the results they expect from those expenditures.

I find it useful to think of paid marketing as the fertilizer and irrigation water that an organization purchases and uses in order to help its crops reach their optimal quality. If we were operating an indoor farm, then conditions would be tightly controlled and we would know the exact type and amounts of fertilizer and water needed to achieve the desired results. If marketing were as direct as indoor farming, then organizations wouldn't at all be hesitant to invest in fertilizer. However, our "farms" don't operate in controlled environments—they operate in the great outdoors.

In the outdoors, fertilizers don't work so tidily. There are mitigating and often unforeseen factors, such as the amount of rainfall the crops receive. Temperature has a substantial impact. Pollination may be impacted by changes in the local bee populations. A neighboring farm may be siphoning off resources from your farm. Wind may be spreading unwanted insecticides onto your crops. The point is that marketing activities can yield significant positive impact but those impacts can be impossible to predict with perfect accuracy—and are incredibly difficult to attribute with precision.

Because its impact can be hard to attribute with precision, many individuals within organizations just feel that paid marketing isn't worth it. There always are other important things that could be done with the money, after all. I have had to defend paid marketing budgets very, very many times in my career, and just as often as not, those budgets would be determined by a process that was more political than financial. In other words, the CFO or CEO would say, "This is all there is for marketing. We need more for another department. So just make it work."

Of course, this spend-what's-left-over approach to budgeting is far from uncommon, but the main point is that paid marketing nearly always looks like a waste of money in the eyes of at least a few leaders within any organization. This state of affairs increases the value of the DEEP Marketing framework due to its transparency. It lets everyone in the organization peer behind the marketing curtain. If DEEP Marketing can help non-marketers get a clearer idea of how marketing is engineered to work for their organization, then marketing budgets should be less vulnerable.

The battle lines that define the debate regarding the efficacy of paid marketing are old and they are deep. However, the debate has taken a bold turn recently. Namely, we have seen how the desire to map the impact of each marketing dollar has, in large part, fueled the rocketlike rise of online marketing—paid search in particular.

## Paid Search Engine Marketing

As defined here, paid search engine marketing (SEM) includes pay-per-click listings that appear on the search engine results pages of Google and the other search engines, such as Bing, Yahoo! and Baidu. I am omitting YouTube (which happens to be the second most searched platform) and Amazon (which is the number one shopping search platform) here because they serve a narrower type of search purpose.

The rapid ascendancy of paid SEM is a very complex story. In order to fully appreciate how to apply DEEP Marketing in paid SEM, it's important that we first look at how the channel works, how it came to be, its strengths and weaknesses, and how the channel is continuing to evolve. Let's begin by

## Using DEEP Marketing in Paid Media Channels

describing how online search engines function, from the perspective of marketers.

When you enter a word, phrase or company name on a search page, the results you receive on the search engine results page (SERP) are a blend of paid listings and organic listings tailored and served specifically to you. *Organic* results are free listings. Free, that is, to the advertiser. In fact, organic listings are what Google and its predecessor, Yahoo!, were originally created to provide—thereby making the world wide web more searchable for users. And in a strict sense, they have achieved that goal.

When you or I are looking for something on Google, we type or speak what we are searching for, hit enter, and then Google returns to us a massive list of web pages where we are likely to find the information we're looking for. It's important that we pause to consider just how massive. For example, when I search for the "Best Thai food in San Diego," Google shares its results with me in about one second. Amazing. In fact, Google tells me right up at the top of the SERP that it found 16.6 million results. That's right, for "Best Thai food in San Diego" there are 16.6 million results. But wait, is it even conceivable there could be 16 million relevant things to be said about Thai food in San Diego?

Right off the bat, I wonder, "How many of these results are even remotely relevant? And how many years would it take me to sort through those millions of results?" I suppose the point is moot because Google also sorts the results for me so the most "relevant" results appear first. They provide this service for free, which is also amazing. As mentioned, the SERP includes a mix of organic and paid listings. Paid ads will appear at the top of the SERP in most cases, with the non-paid listings further down the page. We will look at organic (non-paid) search in the next chapter. For now, we will focus on paid SEM, which is, remarkably, a relatively new advertising mechanism.

Paid ads were quite recently something of a novelty on Google. Before 2000, every listing on Google was an unpaid listing. In the early 2000s, when they were first introduced, paid search ads were very clearly marked as such and could be identified very easily by users. The ads were all neatly corralled in a separate, yellow-colored section of the SERP. For users, it was easy to discern whether they were looking at a paid listing or not. In that respect, it

*127*

*DEEP Marketing*

was like watching a program on commercial television. When the ads come on, it's almost always very clear. You can watch the ads if you'd like, or you can ignore them while you stretch your legs or grab a snack.

Being a Google user for decades, I tended to avoid clicking on paid listings in those early days. I trusted Google to provide me with the most relevant results within their organic listings. Including a paid advertising section on the results page seemed like a very fair way for Google to monetize its investment in its search platform. But as the years have clicked by, paid ads have been taking over the SERPs and—more importantly—they have been styled incrementally in a manner that makes them appear less like ads (see Figure 8).

*Figure 8*

## Paid Search Styling (2007 to 2019)

**2007**
Sponsored link
**View Our Huge Inventory Online**
www.example.com  Example offers unparalelled service and selection. Visit us today.

**2014**
View Our Huge Inventory Online
[Ad] www.example.com
Example offers unparalelled service and selection. Visit us today.

**2017**
View Our Huge Inventory Online
[Ad] www.example.com
Example offers unparalelled service and selection. Visit us today.

**2019**
Ad - www.example.com
View Our Huge Inventory Online
Example offers unparalelled service and selection. Visit us today.

In 2021, the only distinction between a paid listing and an organic listing is the word "Ad" which is written in black and in a font size that's smaller than the listing copy. The visual distinction between paid and organic listings has been nearly obliterated for users.

The conflation of paid and organic listings is alarming—at least as far as the Federal Trade Commission is concerned. The FTC issued guidance in 2002, and again in 2013,[19] advising the search engine companies to make changes to their sites in order to make it easier for consumers to identify paid ads as such. The guidance from the FTC has no teeth though and the search engines have seemingly bypassed the advice.

Whereas Google's original search pages were billed as credible and impartial representations of the web's content, they have long since become a fog of results. If, for example, you perform a Google search for "online degrees" your entire screen will be filled with ads. The SERP will have the general appearance of unbiased search results but it will mostly be ads. You will have to scroll down a bit before you get to any organic results.

The resulting situation is great for those advertisers who can afford to place their ads up top. But it's less than great for the user because now users have to apply their own mental filters to discern the paid ads from the organic listings. And if it's slowly becoming less than great for the consumer, then it's probably only a matter of time before it gets worse for the vast majority of us who are trying to reach the consumer. Nonetheless, as there is tremendous value in getting their listings placed at the top of the SERPs, organizations have been pouring money into paid search.

In fact, paid SEM has become the largest component of paid marketing in record time. For many organizations, it is the single largest category of media expense. The growth of paid SEM is unparalleled in the history of media. Ad revenues for Google have grown from $70 million in 2001 to $147 billion in 2020. That's a little more than two hundred thousand percent

---

[19] Federal Trade Commission. (2013, June 25). *FTC Consumer Protection Staff Updates Agency's Guidance to Search Engine Industry on the Need to Distinguish Between Advertisements and Search Results.* https://www.ftc.gov/news-events/press-releases/2013/06/ftc-consumer-protection-staff-updates-agencys-guidance-search

growth in 20 years.[20] And while it took the television industry more than 50 years to reach $100 billion in ad revenues, it took paid search only 15 years.[21] Google currently earns about $440 million daily on its paid search business. Every. Single. Day.

What else is remarkable about the rise of paid search, and in sharp contrast to the jaw-dropping revenue, is that the medium itself is so stunningly sterile. While television, radio, print, social and online display accommodate a tremendous degree of creativity, art and nuance, paid search serves more as a creative straitjacket. Paid search allows for the narrowest degree of creativity of any medium, yet it has been growing the fastest.

How is this possible?

Throughout the history of commercial media, revenue growth tracked largely with a medium's ability to host richer and more nuanced content. Radio advertising took market share from print. Television advertising took market share from radio. Yet here we have paid search, a medium where one's hands are tied creatively, and it is growing by leaps and bounds.

How have the search engines been able to make so much money on an advertising medium that offers so little creative elbow room? Let's take a look at what Google itself advises in its official guide on how to "Create Effective Search Ads."[22]

> Successful marketers need to deliver the right messaging for the right moment. Better creative messages improve ad relevance and drive more qualified clicks from your Search ads.

---

[20] Statista. (2021, February). *Advertising revenue of Google from 2001 to 2020*. https://www.statista.com/statistics/266249/advertising-revenue-of-google/

[21] Galbi, D. (n.d.) *U.S. advertising expenditure data.* Purple Motes. Retrieved July 1, 2021, from https://www.purplemotes.net/2008/09/14/us-advertising-expenditure-data/

[22] Google Ads Help. (n.d.). *Create effective Search ads.* Retrieved, July 1, 2021, from https://support.google.com/google-ads/answer/6167122?hl=en

## Using DEEP Marketing in Paid Media Channels

Further down the same page, Google includes the rationale for its many best-practice guidelines. Here are several:

- Users tend to engage with ads that appear most relevant to their search.
- Generic calls to action often show decreased engagement with ads.
- Longer headlines increase the clickable space of your Search ads, but you might find that shorter headlines perform better for people already searching for your brand.
- Ads with multiple extensions often perform better than ads with only one extension. They add useful info for searchers and help your message get noticed.
- Multiple versions give you more options to succeed in each auction.
- Many ad formats are about driving more impressions, clicks, and conversions. It's not just about an ad's clickthrough rate.
- Ads optimized to drive clicks can improve your competitiveness in auctions.

Notice that throughout Google's comprehensive guide (which, in its limited scope, is indeed quite useful), the ultimate measure of success is "ad performance." So, to be clear here, Google defines your success as a click on your ad. But a click is the very thing Google sells. Advertisers pay Google for every click someone makes on their paid listings. Some highly competitive keywords have an average cost-per-click of more than 50 dollars.[23]

It's a delicate balancing act for Google, but what they are saying is that in order for your marketing to be a success, you must write ad copy that generates clicks. And, by the way, clicks are what Google sells.

That's right. Google doesn't directly define your success in terms of how well *your* organization's revenue is performing. Google is defining your orga-

---

[23] Statista. (2020, October). *Most expensive keywords in Google Adwords Advertising as of June 2017.* https://www.statista.com/statistics/195680/share-of-keywords-prices-in-google-adwords-advertising/

*131*

nization's success by how well *their own* revenue is performing. We are all expected to make the leap of faith that any click driving someone to our web property is going to put money back into our pockets.

Now, to be clear, Google does encourage organizations to tie their website conversion data (such as purchases made, lead forms completed, email signups, and social shares) back into their bidding and optimization processes. Google actually works very hard to help organizations link their clicks to their revenue. But you and I know a website visit doesn't pay our bills. We also know there are many ways, besides a search engine, to bring visitors to our websites and to our organizations.

To a technologist, the paid search model makes sense: clicks bring visits, some of those visits bring revenue, and therefore clicks bring revenue. But to a marketer, I see the model more as a block of Swiss cheese. I love Swiss cheese. But, wow, it's so full of holes.

Google has come up with an amazing platform providing incredible amounts of data for its advertisers. No wonder we're all spending so heavily here. But cracks may be forming in Google's road ahead. With the potential threat of regulatory changes looming for Google (and for Facebook and Twitter), it may be that paid SEM will look remarkably different ten years from now. Whatever the future holds, DEEP Marketing can help your organization be far more efficient with its paid (and organic) search efforts.

Let's again look at what Google advises. According to Google's own page titled: "Create Messaging that Reflects Your Brand and the Products and Services You Offer," here is what you should focus on when writing paid search ads:

- Create ad text that appeals to users across devices
- Focus on your headlines
- Be mindful of your character limits. You have 30-character headlines, 90-character descriptions, and 15-character URL path fields. Use that space creatively.[24]

---

[24] Google Ads Help. (n.d.). *Create messaging that reflects your brand and the products and services you offer.* Retrieved July 1, 2021, from https://support.google.com/google-ads/answer/6167114?hl=en

## Using DEEP Marketing in Paid Media Channels

Notice that Google's advice is skewed heavily toward the technical: be mindful of device types, focus on headlines, and keep your message within the character limits Google has established. While quite useful to a paid search pro or to a non-marketer, Google's advice here is not by any means advancing the practice of marketing. What the paid search environment has created is a sort of paint-by-numbers version of marketing. In other words, with paid search, now everyone can be a "marketer." We know it can be fun to create a paint-by-numbers artwork, but we also know the resulting canvas is not likely to be adorning any museum walls.

My point here is that we are remarkably constrained with respect to what we can communicate in a paid search ad. I'm not arguing that creativity absolutely cannot exist within the paid search environment. But having to rely on paid search for the lion's share of your marketing is akin to being told you can say whatever you want in your ads—so long as your ads are 300 characters of text or less ... and as long as you don't mind the ads being in a sans serif font in bright blue on a white background. It's just not a satisfactory canvas for a marketer. Something is going to have to evolve. But in the meantime, our hands are somewhat tied.

Nonetheless, DEEP Marketing can help you make the best of the constraints. For paid search, you'll want to restructure your campaigns to align more closely with the Pillars in your DEEP Connector. What you've learned in DEEP Marketing will provide you with a great deal of clarity regarding the types of phrases your potential customers will be using in their searches. This clarity will allow you to abandon no-longer-relevant search query groups and to create more focused query groups.

In addition, DEEP Marketing will allow you to embed more purpose when writing copy for paid search. According to Google, here (see Figure 9) is a template for what makes a good ad:[25]

---

[25] Ibid.

*Figure 9*

View Our Huge Inventory Online | We Carry All
Major Brands | 35 Years of Quality Service
Ad www.example.com/
Example offers unparalleled selection and service. See for
yourself on our official site.

Notice that there are three copy elements featured in the sample headline: huge inventory, major brands, and quality service. Those same three elements are featured in the brief snippet of body copy.

Your organization's headlines should feature the Pillars you identified in your DEEP Connector. Don't lose this focus. The English language is rich, so find as many ways as you can to communicate about your Pillars. Try just one Pillar in some headlines. Try different Pillars in pairs. Try three. Use different combinations of words to describe the Pillars. And as Google suggests, test and test again to see what works best for your organization.

In addition, tie your search ad extensions into your Pillars. Ad extensions are small bits of additional information such as location or product details Google can append to your listing if their algorithms predict that the added text will improve your ad's performance. Extensions can be built manually or you can even let Google automate the extensions so that the words a searcher uses will automatically pop up in your listing like magic. However you decide to handle your extensions, make certain they all tie into and reinforce your Pillars.

Paid search could be seen as just another cost of doing business in the 2020s. But rather than letting your digital agency or the search engines themselves determine what your ads should say, make sure you are in control by ensuring every bit of your search ad copy and your campaign designs are customized to your DEEP Marketing findings.

Another important piece of advice regarding paid search is that you should be prepared for an uphill battle when it comes to how tightly you can control your ad copy and campaign structure. Google is out to make money. We all are. But, if Google's algorithms learn that more money can be made

## Using DEEP Marketing in Paid Media Channels

by favoring your competitors' ads over yours, that is what will happen. In other words, the control is not in your hands. You have an extremely limited degree of control. And as time passes, you are likely to have less control for any given amount of money.

Before leaving the discussion on paid search, let's take a quick look at how mobile and voice search are continuing to change the landscape in SEM. Over time, the percentage of internet searches performed on a mobile device (as opposed to desktop and tablet) has shot up from less than 10 percent in 2012, to 50 percent in 2016, and leveling off around 55 percent between 2019 and 2021. Mobile devices have smaller screens and are more likely to be used in a vertical format as opposed to desktops which have large screens and are dominantly used in a horizontal format. Because mobile searches have been taking market share from desktop searches, the search engine companies are placing more importance on how search performs in a mobile environment. They have shifted to a "mobile-first" approach.

Also note that whereas Google's North American search engine market share has held at between 89 and 92 percent since 2010, its mobile search market share hovers closer to 95 percent.[26] Google absolutely dominates mobile search. Consequently, they are investing more in mobile and continue to update their guidance to advertisers to focus more on mobile.

As mobile continues to dominate the search landscape, make sure your organization considers the way its paid search efforts connect with mobile searchers. For example, ensure your organization's physical presence (if it has one) has been set up in Google My Business. Google My Business allows you to manage your online presence through Google search and Google Maps. In addition, you can allow for customer reviews of your business and a place for you and your customers to upload photos of your business.

The other big mover in paid search is voice search. As with mobile searches, voice searches tend to be performed by individuals who have a more specific and urgent need than those doing desktop searches. Voice searches also tend to contain more search terms since searchers are more likely to be

---

[26] Statcounter. (n.d.) *Search Engine Market Share Worldwide.* Retrieved July 1, 2021, from https://gs.statcounter.com/search-engine-market-share

*135*

using natural language. Advertisers using paid search should be aware that the typically longer voice search phrases create opportunities with respect to pursuing long-tail keyword phrases. They also create opportunities to embed more structured data on your site so that very specific search questions can be answered.

The insights your organization will have learned via the DEEP Marketing process will help you (and your digital agency) tremendously as you consider how to evolve your specific paid SEM tactics to connect better with mobile and voice search users.

## Paid Online Advertising

Whereas paid SEM provides frustratingly little creative room, other forms of paid online advertising offer a fairly expansive platform for creativity in advertising. In online environments, an organization can run ads in the form of video, audio, animation and still images. In many ways, though, there isn't enough control over the medium. It's a bit like the Wild West, so there is a lot to be aware of in order to keep your organization from wasting its money in online advertising. Let's look first at the advantages, then the disadvantages to see how DEEP Marketing can help your organization leverage the upside and avoid the downside.

As far as advantages are concerned, online generally offers better targeting than offline advertising. Online typically offers a lower cost, as well. While cost is always important, targeting is online's most important strength. In fact, the granularity that online can offer is incredible.

Through the online ad serving platforms, you can narrow your audience down by location, behavior, demographics, interests and connections. For example, you can set up your ad campaign in such a way that your ads are only served to men aged 40–44 who are not in a relationship, who follow the NBA, have a college degree and who work in sales, etc, etc. Such finely granular targeting capabilities simply cannot be offered via offline platforms.

Google, in addition to its search functions, offers a powerful online display advertising platform. Google can offer an advertiser the ability to target potential customers by demographics, by location, and by search behaviors. For example, your organization can target people who are in the process of searching for a product similar to yours. You can target people who have been looking for products that are substitutes for your products. Or, if you wish, you can just let Google do the targeting for you based upon its massive stores of data.

Targeting also extends to various device types. Smart TVs and external streaming devices let you target television audiences with your advertising content. Whereas it used to cost substantial sums of money to reach potential customers through their televisions, now it can be done far less expensively and in a more selective manner.

In addition to the targeting capabilities that online offers, you can also test your ads on different audiences. You can adjust age ranges. You can tinker with an endless array of levers in order to improve your results. You can apply findings from one audience to other audiences. You can add clarity to the marketing personas that your organization wishes to connect with. The possibilities seem endless.

Further, pay-per-click models seem to provide a more equitable way to charge advertisers when compared to offline advertising. Whereas the offline world can offer an advertiser a reasonably defined audience, online can offer something more precise. The precision of such models are more eagerly embraced by CFOs, who strive to quantify more precisely the value of your marketing activities. Unfortunately, and as is the case with most anything, there are a number of disadvantages that can offset the advantages. The two primary weaknesses of paid online media relate to: (a) clutter, and (b) lack of transparency.

The word "clutter" may be the best descriptor for the online environment of the early 2020s. The profusion of ads that we encounter online is truly overwhelming—and it's only getting worse. So, why is this the case? The main reason for the clutter is that hosting ads is a way for website owners to earn revenue. This revenue model is true of nearly all mass media. Newspapers, radio and television all relied upon paid advertisers to help make their businesses profitable. Ad revenue has always been an important alternative to subscription revenue in the mass media.

Today, anyone who owns a website can add a simple plug-in to their site which will enable the site to host ads and earn revenue. If you can find ways to increase the number of users visiting your site, and if you can increase the amount of time that those users spend on your site, you can generate more ad revenue. Many websites are built primarily to do just that—make ad revenue for the website owner. Such sites don't exist to support an external business entity. They aren't selling products or services. In these cases, the website-as-ad-server is the business.

The problem with such sites is that the best way to increase ad revenue isn't necessarily to solve people's problems or provide quality content. One frustratingly common way to increase ad revenue is to flood your website with ads in a manner that intentionally makes it difficult for the site visitor to actually find the content they were hoping to find when they were directed to your site.

Try searching for a recipe online. You are likely to be directed by your search engine to an assortment of websites where you will be pelted with ads. The recipe you seek is likely to be buried far down the page, requiring you to keep scrolling down while even more ads pop up, generating revenue for the website owner. In fact, if you have an older computer or browser version, it's not uncommon for the avalanche of ads to freeze your browser, creating the antithesis of a user-friendly experience.

Obviously, there is a balance to be struck. An ad here and there is fine. We all need to make money. But creating and promoting sites solely to generate ad revenue—even at the expense of the user experience—is not a sustainable business practice. Many will argue that the free market will rectify any imbalance here. In other words, if those spammy sites with too many ads repel users, then users will abandon those sites. I don't disagree with the logic, but I also know the searchable web is not a free market and where money can be made, someone will be looking for loopholes through which to do so.

In the prior chapter, I pointed out that Americans (in 2020) were exposed to an average of around 600 ads every waking hour. The vast majority of those ads appear in the online environment. In the meantime, marketers continue to shift dollars toward online advertising, which will only make the digital clutter worse.

## Using DEEP Marketing in Paid Media Channels

As far as DEEP Marketing is concerned, clutter is just another reality to be managed. Carefully consider the value of placing ads that will potentially appear in highly cluttered environments. Also, when evaluating creative concepts, review them amongst a field of other ads. Always be asking whether your ads will stand out within a cluttered environment. If they don't, then consider modifying them or abandoning them for another tactic.

Clutter, however, isn't the only significant defect in the online advertising ecosystem. Transparency is a second major fault. The online environment enables users to cloak their identities—which is a good thing for users. We should all be able to consume content anonymously if we wish. There are a wide variety of actions a user can take to protect their privacy. For example, users can install ad blocking software. They can use virtual private networks to obscure their identity and their location. Users can even create fictitious profile data or email aliases in an attempt to protect their privacy. Again, these are all legitimate behaviors for consumers of online content to pursue.

The effect upon advertisers, however, is that their ads will regularly be served to the wrong users, resulting in a lack of transparency for advertisers. In other words, the audience you are reaching isn't exactly the one you are being sold. The vaunted laser targeting of online advertising isn't truly laser-like. It's not a shotgun but its accuracy is imprecise, despite the impression we are being given. In addition to these somewhat forgivable transparency challenges, there is ample evidence of malicious transparency activity in the pay-per-click (PPC) environment in the form of click fraud.

Click fraud describes the various activities where people or bots are clicking on ads in order to cheat the system. There are two main sources of click fraud. First, if a website earns money each time a visitor clicks on an ad that it hosts, then there is a financial incentive for the owner of said site to inflate the number of clicks, thereby earning themselves more ad revenue. Obviously, the search engines and ad platforms work very hard to identify and stop this type of click activity.

On the other side of the coin, competitors may find it desirable to click on my organization's ads in order to drain my PPC ad budget. This activity, too, is moderately policed. But in any case, the police are often a step behind, so

*139*

you can count on a portion of your online advertising budget to be wasted in these ways. Unfortunately, it just goes with the territory.

Advertisers need to continually ask, "Am I really reaching the audience I think I am buying?"

A third transparency-related weakness involves the fact that when you buy ads through ad networks, you won't know exactly where your ads are running. You will know your ads are being targeted toward users per your specifications but you won't necessarily know what websites the ads will be served through. What you can do is blacklist websites where you don't want your ads to appear. For example, as an advertiser, you can bar your ads from appearing on sites by category (such as pornography or gambling sites) and you can specify websites by name or IP address (for example, to keep your ads from running on competitors' sites or on competitors' networks).

Giving online ad servers the control to run your ads per your audience parameters leaves a lot to chance. Imagine if your political organization's ads appear on a news site right next to a news article on corruption in government. In such a case, the problem isn't solely that your ad is appearing in an unflattering location. The problem is also that you probably will never know your ad appeared there. Your online ad placements, therefore, may be causing you unknown reputational damage.

Transparency and clutter are likely to get worse for advertisers in the foreseeable future. So, while online marketing indeed offers tremendous targeting opportunities, there are a lot of potential downsides—many of which are likely to occur outside of your view. These are risks that need to be better understood and managed. Fortunately, DEEP Marketing can help you make the most out of the upside that online offers and it can help you manage the downside.

To make the most of the advantages of online advertising, your creative assets should be tailored to a highly targeted audience. It makes good sense. If online can provide you with a variety of sharply defined audiences, then each ad you run should be tailored to each of those audiences. If you can

## Using DEEP Marketing in Paid Media Channels

build separate audiences for separate geographic areas, then you can also customize two slightly different versions of your copy to resonate more effectively with each.

To avoid the downsides of online, your ads must be designed with an awareness of the cluttered environment. In other words, they must be boiled down to their simplest form. Content must load quickly. Calls to action must be crystal clear. Taking these simple steps will improve your ability to compete in a most challenging space.

Your DEEP Connector will be invaluable here as you will have narrowed your communication vocabulary to a small set of context-rich words and phrases. The cluttered online ad environment demands brevity and clarity. The evolving dominance of mobile platforms demands brevity and clarity. Fortunately, your DEEP Connector is all about brevity and clarity and will serve you well.

### Paid Social Advertising

The social media platforms are similar to the search platforms in that they offer both organic marketing coverage and paid coverage. As we did with SEM, we will discuss paid social in this chapter and discuss organic social in the next.

Paid social marketing is similar in many ways to other forms of paid online marketing. Advertisers can run ads on Facebook, Twitter, Instagram, LinkedIn, Reddit, YouTube, Snapchat, Pinterest, TikTok, the list goes on. And like other forms of online advertising, paid social allows for incredibly narrow audience targeting, with each platform offering its own strengths, weaknesses and unique audience appeal. In addition, paid social allows advertisers to insert their messaging directly into the content streams of social media platforms. This is the key advantage social offers.

When content is served in a social feed, it's not visually as disruptive as an online display ad. It is therefore more difficult to notice that a snippet of digital real estate is an ad when it's on social media. This is quite important. Think about how we experience ads in most environments. Our eyes, ears and brains are fairly practiced at discerning an ad from what is not an ad. In fact, when we notice something is an ad, we tend to observe it through a more guarded filter.

Americans are somewhat suspicious of ads. And we are becoming more suspicious. Research shows that 47 percent of adults use at least one form of ad blocking in their browsing habits in 2019.[27] We are getting sick of seeing so many ads. This is not to say we don't want to see any ads. We just don't like being bombarded with them.

In a social feed, the ads roll along in a manner just like the posts of those whom we follow. People can comment on the ads and like them or share them. The ad content behaves very much the same as the organic content. Yes, the more savvy users can spot most paid social content but a huge percentage of users can't and don't even think to care.

Obviously, this is a double-edged sword. As users, we all want to be able to discern paid content from organic. But as advertisers, we are kind of okay with things being a bit blurry. I'm sure some advertisers are even ecstatic that users can't tell the difference. In any case, paid social offers a powerful mechanism for reaching, engaging and converting potential customers into paying customers.

So, how does DEEP Marketing inform how to use this marketing channel? As we saw with the paid search platforms, the social platforms also offer their advertisers a laundry list of recommendations on how to generate clicks and engagement. Remember, digital platforms make money by selling clicks, so they are more than eager to offer clear advice that, if followed, should garner clicks. Any well reputed digital agency can help your organization get set up to run paid social campaigns in little time. You can also do it yourself by following the troves of free advice available online.

The advice you hear will sound something like this: define your audience as specifically as possible; define your business goals; set a budget; create ad assets that can be tweaked in ways to accommodate testing; and then test, measure, adjust and repeat.

---

[27] McCue, TJ. (2019, March 19). *47 Percent Of Consumers Are Blocking Ads.* Forbes. https://www.-forbes.com/sites/tjmccue/2019/03/19/47-percent-of-consumers-are-blocking-ads

This all has the appearance of being a very rational process, but the problem is that most organizations don't do a great job of defining their audience. Nor do most organizations do a great job of developing smart creative alternatives for testing. Consequently, audiences aren't targeted as efficiently as they should be, and creative assets are just spat out without a lot of thought. There's a lot of spaghetti being thrown against the wall to see what sticks.

The allure of A/B testing in paid social marketing is strong. Think about it: you can just throw two different creatives out there and test to see which generates the most traffic or the most conversions on your site. After running your test long enough to gather statistically significant results, you can apply your remaining budget behind the winning alternative. However, it isn't hard to see this is a very slippery slope. After all, in testing, you aren't solely determining which creative option performs better, you are also spending money on the weaker creative option while testing. The very real danger is that we are putting any old horse in the test ring. And you should never put any old horse in the test ring. You should only be running your best horses against each other.

I believe the A/B testing framework is valuable—but only if it's employed correctly. You must understand and be okay with the fact that your potential customers will be exposed to your losing creatives as well as your winners. So, do everything you can to ensure even your "losers" are still very good. Don't test average ideas in order to find the better-than-average ideas. You want to test great ideas in order to identify the fantastic ideas. While this advice may sound to many readers as obvious, I feel compelled to share it because it is abundantly apparent that many advertisers are letting their testing be managed by technical people rather than by marketers.

DEEP Marketing provides you with a much clearer idea of who your audience is; and your DEEP Connector arms you with a highly targeted vocabulary to use in your communication. These insights will help you make the most out of the shifting opportunities that the social platforms provide.

## Paid Offline Advertising

Comprising TV, radio, outdoor, print, and direct mail, offline advertising (as it has come to be known since the ascendancy of online advertising) represented the largest marketing expense for the vast majority of organizations prior to the year 2000. However, the meteoric rise of online advertising in the first two decades of the twenty-first century has caused offline advertising to shrink in relative and absolute terms. The reason for the decline in offline media is due largely to the fact that most organizations allocate a fixed amount for marketing. So in order to take advantage of online opportunities, they reduce their offline budget.

Another reason for the major shift away from offline marketing is that the ways we consume media have changed. Televisions originally received their content exclusively via the airwaves, and then via a cable offering a mere dozens of channels. Today, televisions are connected to the internet and can serve online content from a seemingly unlimited number of sources. The same is true for radio.

The most significantly disruptive device, however, is in our pockets. Other than "1-900" telephone services, pretty much zero paid content was consumed on telephones before the smartphone came along. Since the advent of the smartphone, we now gorge ourselves on a feast of content through our mobile devices.

Given these substantial structural shifts in the media landscape, one might think offline media would be dead. But for many organizations, offline remains a major marketing expense. Let's look at how offline paid advertising can be aligned with your findings in DEEP Marketing.

First, there is a wealth of research showing that consumers are more likely to act when they are exposed to messages in a wide array of channels. Known as multi-channel marketing, advertisers typically prefer to deliver their messages in a variety of formats and settings. And while the online environment itself offers a wide array of channels, the content is nonetheless consumed via a very limited number of devices. Therefore, it is wise for advertisers to jailbreak their messages.

To that end, offline provides a way to connect with potential customers in ways that don't involve a smartphone, tablet or computer. While, yes, we are all spending a tremendous amount of time interacting with our personal electronic devices, there are still countless important moments when a potential customer isn't staring at a screen. Recall that in the Discover phase of DEEP

*Using DEEP Marketing in Paid Media Channels*

Marketing we performed a thorough analysis of our competitive environment. In doing so, we identified a number of angles from which our organization could connect with potential customers in nontraditional ways or in unexpected settings. For example, in Chapter 13, we noted that a hypothetical marketer of healthy prepared foods could profitably engage with prospective customers at child safety-themed events.

Television, radio, outdoor and print offer the ability to connect with audiences at home; during their commutes to and from work; or while out of the home shopping, dining or engaging in various recreational activities. In this sense, offline provides opportunities to augment or reinforce your online media presence in ways that support the Pillars in your DEEP Connector.

Another important differentiating aspect of offline media is that you can get much more grand in your creative executions. It's difficult to make a creative statement online when there is so much clutter, when the physical parameters of ad units (ad size, file size, etc.) are so narrowly restricted, and when time spent on any given website can be just a few seconds. Offline, in contrast, can allow you to create huge outdoor installations. Print also offers the ability to do larger executions. Direct mail can let you physically place something in the hands of your target customer. There is a lot of opportunity in these traditional channels.

Lastly, consider that for outdoor media (billboards and transit exteriors, in particular), your message must be designed to be comprehensible in a matter of only a few seconds. People can't read a lot of copy on a billboard or a moving bus or light rail train. Your message must be clear and you should not expect the message will do its job upon one single exposure. Of course, the assumption in using outdoor is that your overarching media plan will expose your target audience to your message many times and, over time, the message will begin to stick. Still, the concise language from your DEEP Connector will help you immensely in developing creative assets that will perform in outdoor media in ways that your competitors may not be able to rival.

◆ ◆ ◆ ◆

Paid advertising can be costly and it comes with some risk. This has been true for as long as paid advertising has existed in any form. As online chan-

*145*

nels continue to pull advertising dollars away from offline channels, marketers are faced with finding ways to make an evolving mix of media perform together well as part of a multi-channel strategy. DEEP Marketing provides a number of clear benefits as organizations continue to navigate these fundamental changes.

CHAPTER 15

# Using DEEP Marketing in Shared and Owned Media Channels

IN THE PREVIOUS chapter it was noted that many organizations harbor a deep-seated reluctance to spending money in paid marketing channels. To the extent that fewer dollars are involved, we find less reluctance with regard to shared and owned media channels. This serves as a double-edged sword, though. On the one hand, shared and owned channels are more likely to be employed by even the most advertising-averse organizations, which is good. On the other hand, since less (or no) money is involved, organizations often use shared and owned channels with less care and intention.

Let's look at these less-expensive channels to see how DEEP Marketing can help add value.

## Shared Media

*Shared Media* encompasses the many opportunities where you can deliver your organization's content via someone else's platform—and in a manner that doesn't appear to be an ad. Sometimes shared media truly is free. Other times, it just appears to be free. In any case, your content, whether it's an ad, or an article, an infographic, or just your organization's name on a banner, doesn't appear to the consumer as an ad. A key reason many advertisers favor shared media is that it can bestow a kind of halo effect. Advertisers can leverage the reputation and reach of an esteemed partner's platform in order to boost their own reputation and reach.

In the first section of the chapter we will look at organic social media. Afterwards, we will examine a second important form of shared media—content marketing.

## Social Media and Content Marketing

While it's not technically difficult to separate paid from organic social marketing, it can be conceptually challenging to do so. Like search, social media started out as an organic-only platform. Google and Facebook provided non-paid platforms that were groundbreakingly disruptive and wholeheartedly embraced by the public. As their numbers of users skyrocketed, the platforms shifted their energies to revenue generation, which, for both, meant selling advertising on their platforms. In one sense, both companies can serve as shining examples of free enterprise. But the shine has been rapidly wearing off.

As both search and social are increasingly driven by their revenue-earning focus, their utility to non-paying marketers continues to diminish. It has become the case for very many organizations that the dominant reason to be on social platforms isn't to connect with the community, but to buy advertising. Nevertheless, non-paid social media can be very effective if managed well.

Social platforms were originally designed and marketed to enable us to share important moments with those who mattered to us. We were able to use social media to share events, photos and videos, humorous content, and emotional content with our friends and families. We can still use it that way for our organizations. But, we should only do so with a plan.

Let's think about the consumer of social media by reflecting upon how you, personally, consume social media. As you scroll through your Facebook, Instagram, LinkedIn or Twitter feeds, you encounter some things that grab your attention and other things that don't grab your attention. Some of the posts grabbing your attention do so in a negative way. In those cases, you may express a disagreeing opinion or even choose to unfollow or block the negative posters. So, for example, if your Uncle Mike is always posting negative or repetitive content, or he's just posting too frequently, you might negatively engage with, or ignore, or even just unfollow him.

*Using DEEP Marketing in Shared and Owned Media Channels*

You need a plan to keep your organization from becoming Uncle Mike. Your organic social posting plan, therefore, should be constructed with three main things in mind:

- Quality
- Timeliness
- Purpose

Specifically, quality refers to content that is concise, error-free, and attention-worthy. Timeliness means that content should be shared with the appropriate frequency and at times when it matters most to your audience. Purpose means that the content should move your audience closer to your organization, whether that is to strengthen, persuade, engage, or convert. Each platform has its own unique set of opportunities when it comes to the elements of quality, timeliness and purpose. For example, according to Facebook's website (which owns Instagram), Instagram is typically better suited to creating awareness whereas Facebook is better suited to creating engagement.

There is so much subtlety and constant change in the organic social media environment that it is usually very wise to work with a digital agency in order to be as up to date as possible. Whether you try to tackle it on your own or with the help of an agency, DEEP Marketing will allow you to think more purposefully about which platforms to use depending upon your audience profiles. It will also help you determine the main themes you will want to highlight in your communication. In other words, you'll want to offer a regular rotation of stories connecting with each of your Pillars.

The same will be true of another form of shared media: content marketing. Content marketing is a hybrid of paid advertising and other forms of non-advertising media. Here are some examples:

- Sponsored content news stories: You'll find all kinds of sponsored content toward the bottom of most news websites. A higher percentage of sponsored content more often corresponds to a lower quality of native news.

*149*

- Infographics: For example, a grocery retailer might develop a useful chart listing the "Best Foods for Boosting the Immune System" in order to increase sales of those products. The retailer may then share the infographic with food and health bloggers who can embed it on their sites and link back to the retailer's product pages for those immunity-boosting foods.
- Movies: Even movies can be a form of content marketing, for example, the Lego movies or the Trolls movies.

Nearly all news media outlets provide advertisers the opportunity to place content on their websites (and in their offline publications) in a quasi-news format. Usually appearing some way down the page, sponsored content will appear mixed in with actual news content. Even the term "sponsored content" is employed (rather than "paid ad") to gently whitewash the source of the content. Some news sites are dominated by sponsored content. Some have very little. But nearly all are devoting more space to sponsored content as each year goes by.

Another place where it is common to see sponsored content is on affiliate marketing-focused blogs. If you do an online search for "Top [fill in the blank]" or "Best [fill in the blank]," you will see a list of sites that are nearly all built around sponsored content. If you search online for the best running shoes, for example, your top search results will consist of articles or blogs—each of which will feature paid ads masquerading as reviews. You're not likely to be reading the impartial and well informed opinions you were searching for. Instead, you'll mostly be reading paid content masquerading as the thing you were hoping to find.

In fact, the hardest aspect of finding the best *anything* online is in wading through the various search results to find a site offering sponsor-free, credible reviews. Why is it so hard to find reliable info? Because there's very little money in providing sponsor-free reviews. There is definitely money to be made in providing sponsor-dominated, ad-based reviews, however. And it's those sponsor-driven sites that are most zealous in following the search engine's recommendations for search engine optimization. As a result, those sites secure the top spots on your search engine results pages.

## Earned Media

The term "earned media" generally refers to news-type stories written directly by organizations who feel they have something newsworthy to share. If those stories are deemed newsworthy by a news entity, then they will be published outright (or with some modification) by those news entities. The word "earned" indicates that the content is truly worthwhile for the publisher to print without charge. In the days before internet publishing, earned media was a far more important component of most organizations' marketing than it is today.

The main reason for earned media's decline in importance is that the mass news media (TV, radio, newspapers) are no longer very highly regarded in the minds of most consumers. According to research from Gallup, the overall reputation of the media has dropped significantly over the last several decades.[28] In the year 2000, about 55 percent of adults in the United States trusted the mass media. In 2020, that figure has dropped to around 40 percent. However, it's very important to note the data hides a sharp divergence between Democratic and Republican adults.

Since the year 2000 in the United States, the percentage of "Democrat" adults who trust the media has actually risen from around 60 to around 75 percent. For "Republican" adults, the story is the opposite, and even more extreme. Since the year 2000, Republicans' trust in the media has dropped from around 50 percent to around 15 percent.

This data shows clearly that your organization's reliance on the mass news media should be measured against whether your target audience is mostly Republican or Democrat leaning. The politicization of "news" over the first two decades of the twenty-first century is a deeply troubling societal development. For marketers though, the trend simply adds greater importance to how much care is taken when segmenting your audience and tailoring messages to those segments. The specificity of the DEEP Marketing framework will help your organization be more effective under circumstances such as these.

---

[28] Brenan, Megan. (2020, September 30). *Americans Remain Distrustful of Mass Media*. Forbes. https://news.gallup.com/poll/321116/americans-remain-distrustful-mass-media.aspx

## Experience Marketing

Another way to leverage shared media is by sponsoring events, other organizations, or causes. Choosing to sponsor or become affiliated with events or causes connecting thematically with your Pillars can allow your organization to be present during key moments in potential customers' lives—specifically, moments when they will be more receptive to embracing your message positively.

For example, if your organization markets office furniture, and your DEEP Connector features *active lifestyle* as a Pillar, then you might choose to be a sponsor at running events. Doing so will connect your organization to the idea of active lifestyle in a space where your competitors are not likely to be present at all.

One fascinating aspect of experience marketing opportunities is that they are often linked to a fan base. Large group activities such as amateur or professional sporting events can be filled with energy and excitement. Many smart marketers have realized there is value in becoming connected with fan energy. The major sports leagues know this and have found ways to monetize their fan bases quite effectively. Consequently, it can be very costly to participate. However, there are many other similar, lower profile events (such as local running races, semi-professional sports, festivals) packing a similar level of on-the-ground excitement and at a much lower cost. Consider how your DEEP Connector might inform how your organization could become affiliated with these types of fan bases.

The overarching strategy with experience marketing is to find ways to connect your Pillars with important moments in your customers' lives and then to be present during those moments. Even though there may not be a direct connection between your organization's product/service category and the event itself, you can share in those important moments and let the glow of that importance solidify your message and reflect positively upon your brand.

*Using DEEP Marketing in Shared and Owned Media Channels*

## Owned Media

In addition to the media channels where we pay or partner in exchange for marketing exposure, organizations also rely on a number of their own channels in order to communicate directly with their customers and potential customers. Typically, an organization's website is its most visible and powerful tool. Email marketing, blogs, newsletters, printed literature and sales language round out this tool bag. Let's now look at how DEEP Marketing helps with these owned channels. Then we will close the chapter by looking at brand assets.

### Web, Organic Search, and Email

An enlightening way to consider how to use your own organization's web assets is to consider the origin of the web and the evolution of the website. Websites are a relatively new thing. Early in my career, I worked for organizations that didn't have websites because the world wide web had not been invented yet. So, I've been a marketer in the pre-web world and have witnessed the many ways that the web has changed, and continues to change, marketing.

The world's first public web page went live in 1991 but things didn't really take off until the mid-90s, when the number of websites online began to creep up into the thousands. By the late 1990s, the world wide web had assumed many of the characteristics of a mania or a gold rush with investors pouring cash into an emerging ecosystem that wasn't very well understood. The tech-focused NASDAQ stock index rose 400 percent between 1995 and 2000—the year of the *dot-com* crash, when the NASDAQ's bubble popped. Many of the large players in those early days lost everything when the bubble burst, though some survived. By 2014, there were more than one billion websites.[29] In short, the web is very young and it has grown explosively.

An interesting feature of explosive growth of any kind is that it doesn't happen without a lot of replication. When something goes viral, it does so by lending itself to being rapidly and easily copied. And true to form, the pre-

---

[29] Internet Live Stats. (n.d.) *Total number of Websites*. Retrieved July 1, 2021, from https://www.internetlivestats.com/total-number-of-websites/

*153*

dominant way to build a website is, and has always been, to copy another website—or at least to copy components of other sites. Due to the forces of easy replication, every website we see today is a not-so-distant copy of a copy of those original websites from the mid-1990s.

Since the 1990s, websites have changed but their evolution has largely been stylistic. The core elements of the vast majority of websites remain consistent: a homepage with hero image, top navigation menu, a hamburger button and search bar in the upper corners, call-to-action buttons on each page, secondary links in the footer, and so on. The website as we know it hasn't yet gone through its chrysalis stage.

Consider this: what is the purpose behind your organization's website? How does it serve your organization? Unless your site is strictly a commerce site, then my guess is that your site serves several purposes. Maybe even too many purposes. And this is all because everyone in your organization has an expectation that your website will meet their particular needs. I've been through the website redesign process many times. Building a new website is awkwardly as much a political exercise as it is a business exercise because the underlying purpose of the website is often nebulous. Recall that today's websites are not-so-distant offspring of the world's original websites. Those original websites lacked a clear purpose and therefore today's tend to, as well. The haziness has become kind of hardwired.

Is the purpose of your site to generate leads? Is the purpose to generate sales? Is the purpose to support current customers' needs? Is the purpose to provide directions and information on operating hours? How about providing leadership bios? Is there a blog? Are there virtual tours? Is the site primarily designed to meet the needs of existing customers or potential customers?

Vagueness is the enemy of efficiency. So, if your site's primary purpose is generating leads, then your site architecture and design need to reflect that very clearly. Unfortunately, the websites of most organizations usually get designed by a committee. Concessions are made to one department at the detriment of another. Clarity and focus lose out. However, the structural quirks of organizations aren't the only things that have muddled website functionality. Neither the search engines pushing traffic to our websites nor

*Using DEEP Marketing in Shared and Owned Media Channels*

the browsers we all use to view those websites are being engineered to improve the effectiveness of our organizations.

Web browsers and search engines have been engineered primarily to optimize their utility to advertisers. The dissatisfying result is that website design to this day is structured largely around ensuring websites achieve two rudimentary objectives—namely: (a) to receive search traffic, and (b) to not break. Everything else comes in a very distant third. So, even though the search engines tell us to focus first on content, it's a disingenuous directive.

I liken the situation to a shopping mall. The world wide web is like a shopping mall so impossibly massive that its visitors must ask the mall management where to find what they are looking for. To keep things running smoothly, the mall managers tells us shopkeepers exactly how to configure our stores in order to direct visitors to us. Sure, we can sell what we want inside our stores. We can paint the walls of our stores however we want. But the core layout of our stores is dictated for us. If we don't lay our stores out like the mall management advises, then we won't receive many (or any) visitors—that is, unless we simply pay the mall management for visitors. That's one guaranteed way to get visitors.

While this highly prescriptive arrangement certainly makes things more efficient for mall management, it's kind of forcing our individual stores to all look alike. And it hinders our individual ability to interact more authentically with our potential customers.

Fortunately, there is a lot we can do to make the best of our less-than-ideal situation. First of all, websites are external facing. Therefore, as is the case with any external communication, our DEEP Connector should dictate what we say on our websites. Our DEEP Connectors should also, to the limited extent possible, inform how our websites function in terms of user experience and in terms of user interface. We should work hard to find ways to make our websites exude the qualities we have chosen to feature in our DEEP Connectors. For example, if one of our Pillars is *fast service*, then our website absolutely must be very fast and efficient.

As far as language is concerned, standard website design lends itself to bold, clear language. Therefore, the language on your organization's website should come directly from your DEEP Connector. The website visitor should

*155*

clearly see that language reflected from the homepage right on through the entire site. Consider your DEEP Connector language when creating: URLs, headlines, call-to-action buttons, thank-you pages, subscription pop-ups and landing pages. Again, using the language from your DEEP Connector is important because you have already determined it is the best language, and because you want to repeat yourself in order to get your message through the noise.

Now, if your organization relies on paid online marketing, you are likely to be employing web landing pages. Not many years ago, advertisers would send their paid online traffic to their website's homepage or to other native pages on their public websites. Around 2010, organizations began building custom landing pages for their search traffic. The thinking behind the shift was due to the emergence of a practice called *conversion optimization*.

Conversion optimization is a process that attempts to measure and minimize the friction separating paid ads from revenue. Recall that the search engines and your pay-per-click ads send traffic to your sites by providing clickable links. In a perfect world, I could follow each ad click in order to see whether it actually "converted" on my site. In other words, did the person complete a lead form or did they subscribe to my email list, or did the person make a purchase. After all, we aren't just paying for website visitors. We are paying for firm leads or sales. We want our website visitors to convert.

When I place a PPC ad, I know I will pay for every click generated by the ad. If I build my site the way the search engines suggest, then I can track those clicks and attribute conversions—such as email signups, or lead forms —to those clicks. I can also set a dollar value for those conversions. The value gets plugged into the algorithms which will then optimize how and when my ads are served so that clicks are more likely to convert on my site. While this sounds great in principle, it falls short in execution.

After all, we are trying to track user activity in order to help us understand attribution and determine which actions are most likely to yield revenue. But there are so unfathomably many data points and so many blind spots in the conversion tracking process that the only way to improve our conversion rates is to keep pouring more data into the search engines' databases. The underly-

## Using DEEP Marketing in Shared and Owned Media Channels

ing premise of conversion optimization is that more data will yield deeper knowledge and better business results for advertisers.

My concern is that we are spending far too much time obsessing about trackable attribution and not nearly enough time focusing on messaging and the myriad cross-channel dynamics impacting conversion. By focusing all of our attention on the minutiae, we risk losing sight of the bigger picture. Activities like conversion optimization absolutely have a place, but their place shouldn't be elevated above other far more important aspects of marketing.

We shouldn't lose sight of the fact that we have been—and still are—designing our websites according to a set of technical parameters that aren't being driven by the needs of our customers or of our organizations. Unquestioning adherence to an out-of-date rulebook invites dysfunction and eventually creates an environment ripe for a new rulebook. On behalf of the marketing profession, I hope someone out there is writing the next rulebook for the web.

Now that we've looked at websites, let's look at how users find those websites via organic search listings. Recall that your visitors aren't the only important readers of your site. The search engines rely on their search bots or crawlers to do the heavy lifting of indexing everything on the web. If you build a new website or if you make changes to your website, the search engines won't just automatically know this. Their crawlers will need to visit your site and scan your new content in order for a web user to eventually find it on a SERP. Since it's a herculean task to read the entire world wide web, the search engines provide generous guidance to web developers on how to help their crawlers discover and make sense of new web content.

The crawlers pay particular attention to key web page elements including sitemaps, menus, header tags, slugs, meta descriptions, snippets, structured data and a lot more. Optimizing your website for the search engine crawlers is a science unto itself. There are tremendously useful resources online that can tell you what the search engines like to see. But since those directives are updated regularly, it's best for you to seek support from a dedicated expert if you are developing new content for your site or particularly if you are building a new site.

*157*

Digital marketing experts tell us paid search and organic search support one another. In a perfect world, your organization should show up in paid and organic form on the SERPs—which implies we are kind of obliged to pay if we want to succeed. But why do we need to pay? One reason is our competitors employ search tactics not only to boost their own organizations, but also to suppress our organizations. In other words, we need to think of search in both offensive and defensive terms. The way this works is that our competitors can use paid search to buy prominent positions on SERPs where people are searching for our organization.

For example, when I do a Google search for "MBA University of Oregon," the SERP lists three other university programs before the listing for the University of Oregon. How an inverted ordering of results is intended to help the search user, I have no idea. How the SERP supports the "most relevant results" credo, I also have no idea. In any case, realize that the search environment deck is stacked against those with smaller marketing budgets. On the other hand, it is stacked in favor of those who can be as specific as possible in defining their audiences and speaking in very precise language. If you don't have the deepest pockets among your league of competitors, then you'll need to rely on your solid marketing core and on your findings in the DEEP Marketing process in order to compete. Clarity can compete quite effectively against cash.

Now let's look at blogs and email marketing. I pair these two because blogs and email marketing usually work in tandem. In our blogs we share routine stories and information useful to our customer family. We also alert our customers via email that we have new content for them to enjoy. With our customer relationship management software, we can then track the responses to those emails and track users' blog visitation, and their eventual conversion status. The email/blog mechanism is an important tool when we consider ways to move potential customers into the actual customer category.

The most common challenge with blogs is that they take a commitment. The entire point of a blog is that its subscribers receive a steady stream of useful information. The steady stream of information provides its own inherent value and it provides a way to engage more deeply with prospective and current customers. Fortunately, the DEEP Marketing process will arm your

## Using DEEP Marketing in Shared and Owned Media Channels

organization with a series of content themes enabling you to talk about topics meaningful to your customer family and to your organization.

Here are several ways to apply your DEEP Connector to your blogs and email marketing activities:

- Write stories based on your DEEP Connector Pillars
- Choose message frequency that is brand appropriate
- Give your blog a name that reinforces your DEEP Connector
- Subscribe language should be informed by DEEP Connector
- Share your blog content on other platforms that align with your Pillars

The worldwide web has changed everything in marketing in the last few decades. But it has also changed nothing. The web has given us a whole new suite of tools and has changed the way we portray ourselves in the world via these strange entities called websites. On the other hand, as marketers, we are still simply trying to persuade people that we have what they need in order to make their lives better. New tools. Same game. And those tools, while new, won't do what you need them to do without the right framework in place.

### Sales and Customer Service Language

In Chapter 3, I stated that a good marketer must constantly be striving for perfect alignment between three phases of the customer relationship:

1. What you promise to a potential customer
2. What the customer experiences at the moment they first contact you
3. What the customer experiences during and after their purchase

Most of the discussion so far in this and the prior chapter has been about that first step: what we promise to a potential customer. The bulk of what we are managing in the Project phase of DEEP Marketing entails what we are promising to potential customers. But the second and third steps are also, of course, vitally important.

Imagine you're in a situation where you have done a spectacular job with the first step (what you promise to a potential customer). That is, you have constructed and delivered a compelling case for why your customer should count on you to solve their problem. The next step in the process is that the customer is going to reach out to you. This means they are going to call you, or visit you in person, or perhaps they will complete an application or even just place an order. In each case, your organization has spent a lot of thought, time and money to get to this magic moment of truth.

If you drop the ball at this point, you will damage—or even lose—your chance of putting this potential customer into the category of actual customer. You should consider all the ways this handoff could go wrong and then put things in place to ensure they don't. The list below shows the many places where you could be inadvertently dropping that baton. You've told them a great story so far. This is the moment when you must begin delivering. Make sure your DEEP Connector informs each of these components in your marketing/sales processes:

- Call center scripts
- Online chat scripts
- Phone support scripts
- On-hold scripts
- Website thank-you pages
- Online ordering forms
- Transaction confirmation emails

Marketers have access to an amazing array of channels via which to engage with customers. Whether your organization is using channels that are paid, shared or owned, it is always the case that you will improve your chances of connecting with the customer if your message is targeted well and if the message is compelling and clear. DEEP Marketing provides a framework allowing you to do so.

## Brand Assets

The final marketing concept I'd like to cover is the one that may be the least well understood: brand. It's remarkable how many definitions of brand there are. And while it's tempting to create yet another definition, what matters isn't that we nail down a correct definition. As we learned in Chapter 3, even the word "marketing" has a number of conflicting definitions. Definitions don't help much when it comes to concepts so pervasively misunderstood. What matters is that we share an understanding here.

So, what is a brand? The first thing to understand is that brand is all about how others see and feel about your organization. I may define myself as being a stylish person, but if my clothes are ill-fitting and out-of-date, then my brand will not be one of stylishness, despite how I wish for others to see me. Likewise, brand isn't what I think about my organization. It's what others think about it. This is the most important thing to understand about brand.

The second most important thing to understand when it comes to brand is that it is pan-dimensional. Brand is influenced by dimensions including what we say, how we say it, when we say it, what we're wearing when we say it, the music playing when we say it, and so on. Brand is a feeling that arises in others based on everything I do and everything I am perceived as being associated with.

Therefore, your brand is not your logo. Your logo is more like an embroidered emblem on a polo shirt. It is only a small, albeit visible, expression of who we want to be. Logos would matter a lot more if we all looked, dressed and behaved exactly the same way. If that were the case, then our logos could kind of define us. They would be the only thing setting us apart from one another. But we aren't all alike. We are all quite a bit different.

Because brand is an amalgamation of many elements, organizations shouldn't lead their communications with narrowly defined brand assets. Brand assets are like empty containers that we employ to carry meaning. A logo isn't sufficient to convey what your organization is even if you spend out-

*161*

rageous amounts of money. So, remember that our most visible brand element—our logos—don't define who we are. Designed thoughtfully, however, they can help us express more clearly who we are.

DEEP Marketing is all about getting to the core of things. So, completing the DEEP Marketing process will provide your organization with the understanding it will need when it comes time to redesign or refresh your organization's brand toolkit. As was the case for other creative assets, your DEEP Connector will provide a great deal of what's needed when developing your brand. For example, brand elements such as your logo, typography, graphics and voice need to be fashioned in a way that reinforce the Pillars in your DEEP Connector.

It also helps to realize there is not only one perfect logo or font or color for your organization. The founder of Nike, for example, ended up choosing the iconic *swoosh* logo without a lot of excitement. It wasn't seen as the perfect logo at the time. It was just the best option available when he needed to commit to one.[30] It became a perfect logo only after being associated with all the meaning that Nike poured into it for so many years. If Phil Knight had chosen a different logo, Nike's success wouldn't have been diminished. We'd just have a different graphic on our shoes.

Therefore, if your organization's DEEP Connector includes *safety* as a Pillar, for example, this doesn't mean you have to choose the one color somehow equating most closely with safety. There are plenty of colors that could be called upon to reinforce the notion of safety. Further, there are few colors that map universally to specific qualities. The color red indicates danger in some cultures, but it signals something quite different in other cultures. And even within cultures, individuals have their own feelings with respect to various colors.

Color is just one of a multitude of brand elements. You need to be aware of the entire picture. The elements of language and tone of voice can be just as important as the visual elements of an organization's brand. Organizations would do well to spend less time obsessing about visual elements and more

---

[30] Marker. (2020, February 28). *Phil Knight on the Surprising Origin Story of Nike's Name and Swoosh*. https://marker.medium.com/phil-knight-on-the-surprising-origin-story-of-nikes-name-and-swoosh-cb37183d5d4f

## Using DEEP Marketing in Shared and Owned Media Channels

time thinking about how their messages are delivered. This particular aspect of brand exemplifies how DEEP Marketing can strengthen your organization's marketing effectiveness.

Here's why.

The first step in DEEP Marketing is an exercise in Discovery. Most organizations don't come close to conducting a thorough job of this. Imagine how much clearer your sense of your organization's self will be after going through the full Discover process of DEEP Marketing. Simply by completing the first step in DEEP Marketing, you will gain a new understanding of why your organization exists, who you exist to help, and how your organization does it in a way like no one else. These are the core elements required for an organization to have true self-awareness. And it is that organizational self-awareness that allows strong brands to be built.

After your organization completes the DEEP Marketing process, you'll find your entire organization will begin exuding your desired brand qualities. Brand management will no longer be relegated to the marketing department's brand standards enforcement team. In this important aspect, DEEP Marketing has the effect of strengthening an organization's brand core enabling the entire organization to communicate and compete more effectively.

♦ ♦ ♦ ♦

As observed throughout this book, we see organizations like we see icebergs. Potential customers can see only the ten percent that's visible above the waterline while the bulk of the iceberg remains unseen and unheard. Unfortunately, for many organizations, the visible ten percent isn't adequately connected with the remaining ninety percent of the organization. Consequently, the messaging that those organizations project out into the world lacks the depth, clarity and purpose required to compete successfully. DEEP Marketing helps organizations rewire themselves so that all of their external communication—whether paid, shared or owned—can deliver superior results.

# Conclusion

I OPENED THIS BOOK by declaring that marketing was broken.

Decades of work in marketing had revealed to me a number of troubling symptoms in my profession. First among the symptoms was the high and unmatched turnover in marketing-related jobs. Second was the rampant lack of creative control in advertising. Third was the ubiquitous lack of messaging consistency among an organization's staff. And fourth was the slow surrender of marketing to big data and AI. These four symptoms suggested to me that there might be a core structural defect creating dysfunction in marketing.

I postulated that the core reason for the dysfunction in marketing was the gap separating how marketers and their non-marketer colleagues in organizations define, understand and approach marketing. I proposed further that the schism wasn't only preventing marketing from functioning optimally for the organization, it was also weakening the entire organization.

My next step was to devise a way to remedy the gap, thereby allowing marketing to function at a more optimal level. I developed a framework to serve as a bridge within organizations. The four-phase DEEP Marketing framework and the DEEP Connector help organizations bridge the disconnect existing between marketers and non-marketers—a gap preventing organizations from being as successful as they otherwise could be.

So, let's review how DEEP Marketing addresses each of the four symptoms.

## Symptom 1: High Turnover in Marketing

Organizations assign far too much power and culpability to individuals in marketing. An organization's marketing presence is too big and too important to be attached to a single individual. DEEP Marketing provides a framework assigning the ownership of an organization's marketing to the organization itself—and not solely to its current marketing leader. In doing so, marketing performance failures are no longer attributed solely to an individual and churn no longer serves as the default approach to fixing issues loosely defined as "marketing" problems.

## Symptom 2: Bad Creative Everywhere

Examples of bad marketing—whether due to sloppy work, vagueness or invisibility—are most often caused by a lack of clarity in purpose when creative assets are being developed. DEEP Marketing provides a framework designed to bring tremendous definition to the messaging and targeting for your marketing efforts. The DEEP Connector will help your organization and its partners to develop creative assets that are tightly focused upon your organization's unique position in the market. A second major cause of bad creative is that non-marketers too often have the ability to derail the creative process for any number of unspecified reasons. The DEEP Connector is also designed to reduce the damage caused by this dynamic.

## Symptom 3: Lack of Message Clarity Among Staff

It is all too common that you'll find a widely inconsistent variety of messages when you ask random staff members what their organization is all about. This lack of consistency: (a) reflects the fact that most organizations define marketing only as the communication coming from the marketing department, and (b) represents a huge missed opportunity in terms of free marketing. The DEEP Marketing process has been specifically designed to arm every member of your organization's staff with the underlying rationale and specific language to share whenever they are talking about the organization. The process also deputizes everyone in your organization to consider themselves as part of the marketing team, and serves as a tool to use when bringing new staff on board.

## Symptom 4: Marketing's Surrender to Big Data

Marketers are increasingly allowing big data and AI to call the shots when it comes to tactical execution in their online marketing. This surrender of control represents unnecessary risk to the organization. The DEEP Market-

## Conclusion

ing process provides a framework that will enable your marketing team to resist the temptation to devote all of its budget to big-data-driven end-of-funnel marketing tactics such as paid social and paid search.

When I set out to create the DEEP Marketing framework, I did so with the sincerest of hopes that the framework would help those organizations struggling with their marketing. I am well aware there is a wealth of excellent marketing advice out there, but I was also aware that the advice wasn't even coming close to fixing the rampant dysfunction in marketing. I eventually realized that what was needed was a solution employing a more holistic approach. Fixing things when they aren't working is not easy. But it helps tremendously to have a well crafted plan. DEEP Marketing is designed to serve as your plan.

If you are ready to give DEEP Marketing a shot, your next question may be, "When is the best time for me to move forward?" Fortunately, there is really no bad time to begin applying DEEP Marketing within your organization. If your organization is showing symptoms, then any time is a good time to begin working on a fix.

As there is no bad time, there is also no perfect time to begin applying DEEP Marketing—unless your organization is just getting off the ground, or unless your competitive or customer environments are in turmoil. In those instances, DEEP Marketing can help to assure lasting benefits at a very key time.

If your organization's marketing efforts can't gain traction, or if you're struggling with any of marketing's symptoms of dysfunction, then DEEP Marketing may be of great help to you and your organization. Strengthening your marketing core will yield positive results in many ways.

♦ ♦ ♦ ♦

In the following Special Section of this book, we will look at how DEEP Marketing can bring even greater benefit to two types of organizations that suffer from their own unique symptoms of dysfunction in marketing: start-ups and nonprofits.

SPECIAL SECTION

# DEEP Marketing for Start-Ups and Nonprofits

CHAPTER 16

# Start-Ups and Young Organizations

AS WE LEARNED in Parts 1 and 2 of this book, DEEP Marketing is a process designed specifically for leaders who want to fix their organization's marketing.

There would have been no need to develop the DEEP Marketing framework had there not been so much evidence that marketing is malfunctioning in so many organizations. But as we have seen, there are a number of symptoms serving as evidence that marketing is not working well for countless organizations: high turnover, ineffective creative, lack of internal messaging consistency, and the surrender to big data.

Most leaders who encounter the DEEP Marketing framework will do so because their organization has been suffering from one or more of these symptoms. Most of these individuals will have invested some time trying to fix things, but will not have found a solution. So, in their quest for a solution, they turn to the DEEP Marketing framework in order to fix a problem that has stalked their organization for years.

But what if your organization is new? Specifically, what if your organization is too new to be pursuing any external marketing yet? Perhaps your organization hasn't existed long enough to experience any outward symptoms of dysfunction. If this is the case, it may not really be possible to know if your marketing is prewired to fail in the not-too-distant future.

While we can't predict how well any given start-up organization will perform, we do know that, in general, new organizations can struggle. Let's take a look at one key symptom of dysfunction that plagues many start-up organizations.

## Symptom: Flawed Marketing is the Number One Reason Why Start-Ups Fail

Imagine for a moment that your vibrant young organization is instead a vibrant young person who decides to take up running and attempt a marathon. Wanting to apply some structure to your efforts, you might opt to start your training by following one of the numerous marathon training programs available online. But because your body is still young and strong, it may be impossible to perceive that your sudden increase in running volume is causing unseen stress and damage to your bones and joints. When you feel a little pain, you're likely to ignore it or think it's normal and will go away on its own.

In fact, it may take a number of months or even years to realize that your running form and core fitness have been mismanaged from the very beginning, and that you are doomed to experience a pattern of recurring injuries that seem impossible to fix. Correcting the problem will require a lot more work than had you gotten your form and fitness right before you began accumulating all those running miles.

The path to dysfunction for a young organization is similar. A new business is launched with great energy and passion. A marketing plan for the new venture is crafted by following one of many credible marketing plan templates available in books or online. External funding is sought but not without encountering more hurdles and rejections than were expected. Funding is eventually secured, but two years later, sales aren't materializing per your lofty projections. A new marketing leader is brought on board. Additional money is spent on marketing. But after another two years, the balance sheet is looking scarier than ever. More funding is needed to keep the doors open, and a success story is increasingly difficult for potential investors to envision given an emerging track record of lackluster performance.

Of course, it is widely known that many new businesses fail. In fact, according to the United States Bureau of Labor and Statistics, 45 percent of new businesses fail within their first five years of operation and only one in four new businesses makes it to its tenth year.[31] It should be safe to presume

---

[31] U.S. Bureau of Labor Statistics. (2016, April 28). *Entrepreneurship and the U.S. Economy.* https://www.bls.gov/bdm/entrepreneurship/entrepreneurship.htm

## Start-Ups and Young Organizations

the vast majority of new business owners are keenly aware their survival is far from guaranteed.

It should also be safe to assume most new business owners perform at least a little research to learn more about why most new businesses fail. Getting to the truth as to why any specific new business fails can be a complicated exercise. After all, businesses usually fail due to a number of interrelated factors. But it is very clear that, in the aggregate, the two primary reasons new businesses don't succeed are: (a) failure to connect with the market, and (b) failure to raise sufficient capital.

Consider further that the most likely reason driving a failure to raise sufficient capital is because the potential providers of capital—venture capitalists, banks, the Small Business Administration—don't have faith in the new business's market opportunity. It is so incredibly important to reflect on this. What's the main reason new businesses fail? Flawed marketing in their infancies.

The single thing you can do to minimize your odds of failure as a new business venture is to get your marketing right at the beginning. Doing so offers the twin advantages of helping you eventually compete in the market, and helping you secure funding.

Therefore, if your organization is just getting off the ground, there is no better time than the present to apply the DEEP Marketing framework. Specifically, there are three main reasons for this:

1. It is far less complicated to get your marketing right at the beginning than it is to untangle a broken marketing structure and rebuild it.
2. A young organization possessing a clearer marketing focus during its infancy is more likely to be successful in connecting with its market and generating earned revenue as it matures.
3. A young organization possessing a clearer marketing focus during its early stages is more likely to secure investment capital.

Let's look first at why a new organization would have an easier time implementing DEEP Marketing than would a more mature organization.

Recall that DEEP Marketing includes four phases: Discover, Elaborate, Embrace and Project. The Discover phase involves a thorough analysis of the market in which your organization operates. In the Discover phase, we examine key aspects of the three primary domains shaping our opportunity in the market. The three domains (or constellations) are the customer family, the league of competitors, and the organization itself. Following the collection of data, we look for meaningful convergences among the three constellations in order to identify our strongest potential position (or positions) in our market.

Market analysis is a necessary activity for any new organization. Therefore, some components of the Discover work may already have been completed by your young organization. And if your young organization hasn't yet completed its marketing research, then the Discover phase of DEEP Marketing provides a perfect launch platform for your marketing research.

Further, founders are, by definition, keenly attuned to the specific needs their organization was designed to address. It is thereby far easier for a young organization to more accurately describe its own passion and market position in the Discover phase. These factors enable you to hardwire the Discover findings into your organization's core more deeply than can a more mature organization that has begun to struggle.

The next two phases in DEEP Marketing are Elaborate and Embrace, both of which involve a high degree of intraorganizational collaboration and team-building. Again, these activities are easier to orchestrate successfully within smaller and younger organizations than in older and larger organizations. Getting a small and highly energetic team on the same page is a vastly simpler task than doing the same with a larger and more rigid group.

This is particularly true for a start-up organization where employees are investing personally in the possibility of future success. Start-ups frequently don't pay much in terms of salary or benefits so their employees are likely to see themselves as owners or shareholders in the organization. Their commitment to success is much higher than what you will find among those in a more established organization. The commitment of the team members in your young organization ensures that it will be far easier to conduct the second and third phases of DEEP Marketing.

## Start-Ups and Young Organizations

The fourth and final step in DEEP Marketing is where we project our newly defined marketing messages out into the world. It would again be easier for a younger organization to implement this step since it is less likely to have a large marketing presence in its early stages. In contrast, it would be more complicated and time consuming for an older organization to work through the Project phase since they would be more likely to have a larger array of communication tactics to adjust.

Now that we have explored why and how it is mechanically easier for a younger organization to implement the DEEP Marketing process, let's look at the far more urgent reasons why a newer organization *should* implement DEEP Marketing—which are: (a) to connect with its market, and (b) to secure capital.

It should go without saying that connecting with one's market is the overarching goal of marketing. Yet it's worth reiterating, because it's too easy to approach one's marketing as a one-way activity flowing from the organization to the world outside. Marketing might be better envisioned as the forging of a bond between the organization and its market. Bonds, however, can be temperamental. They are difficult to establish and to maintain—particularly when one is laboring within a competitive environment. Creating a bond can be far easier to achieve when your organization can establish itself in a position relatively free of competitors.

As we learned in Part 1, marketing is a competitive activity. We are trying to connect with a market within a competitive environment. And to their benefit, young organizations have a special competitive advantage in that they are unknown (for the time being) to their competitors. Their relative invisibility allows new organizations to establish a beachhead from which they can forge bonds with their market and later defend themselves from their competitors. Being small can allow you to create your own special market position and fortify it before your competitors have the opportunity to become aware of your existence. There is tremendous value in creating this type of foundation for your organization. When you consider that the main reason new businesses fail is weak marketing, then it follows that a young organization's best hedge against failure is a strong marketing foundation.

A strong marketing core also allows an organization to avoid the four most glaring symptoms of broken marketing, which are high turnover, bad creative execution, poor messaging consistency throughout the organizational team, and the surrender to big data. As a new organization, you have but a limited amount of time before you run out of funding and are forced to close your doors. DEEP Marketing will help your young organization avoid the traps of marketing dysfunction and help you survive and eventually grow.

## Using DEEP Marketing to Help You Raise Start-Up Capital

Finally, let's look at how DEEP Marketing will help a newer organization secure financing. For the most part, start-up investors are looking for strong financials paired with compelling stories of potential success. The DEEP Marketing process will improve your chance of fundraising success by:

- Helping you to build a more meaningful and focused pitch
- Getting your leadership team completely aligned on language
- Demonstrating you've performed a thorough analysis of your market opportunity

As described in Chapter 10, the DEEP Marketing process includes a step where you prepare a superpower presentation deck to share with your staff. The outline of that same presentation deck can serve as the backbone of your pitch deck by making the following modifications:

1. Your organization has performed a thorough analysis of: (a) its potential customers, (b) its competitors, and (c) itself, in order to identify opportunities for success. The analysis uncovered a number of key findings.
2. Describe your key findings.
3. The nexus where the key findings converge describes our organization's unique place in the market. It is our organization's superpower.

4. Frame your superpower in the following terms: "People are suffering because an important need isn't being met very well. Our organization is wired to meet this need exceptionally well, and in a way no one else does."

A pitch deck will, of course, include a great deal more information including the potential size of the market opportunity, financial projections, and key personnel profiles. Nonetheless, the clarity and rigor with which you demonstrate your knowledge of the marketplace, your competitors, and your role within it, can form the hook that will spur interest in your venture. Your financials, certainly, have the power to break your case. But without a solidly grounded and compelling marketing narrative, a set of rosy financials may not, on their own, be sufficient to make your case either.

Further, the DEEP Marketing process will help you to ensure that everyone on your small team will be perfectly aligned on message. Recall that message inconsistency can be a killer in terms of an organization's marketing effectiveness. Message inconsistency can also be a killer when it comes to pitching an investor. DEEP Marketing will allow you to project a rock-solid messaging front to your prospective investors.

The DEEP Marketing model was designed to function as a guide to help leaders fix an organization's broken marketing. DEEP Marketing can also function as a guide to help leaders of new organizations create a solid marketing core that will help their organization compete early, secure the financing it needs, and avoid the symptoms of marketing dysfunction haunting so many older organizations.

# CHAPTER 17

# Nonprofit Organizations

DEEP MARKETING WAS DEVELOPED primarily to support the needs of organizations that need help fixing their marketing—no matter the type of organization. But, as is the case with start-up organizations, DEEP Marketing also conveys special benefits to the leaders of nonprofits.

Having worked in nonprofits for about 30 years, I know very well that their marketing and communications efforts face a complex array of challenges. Let's examine the unique symptoms of dysfunction and the obstacles confronting nonprofits as they pertain to marketing. We will start on a more strategic level and then work our way down to tactics. In addition, let's explore the ways DEEP Marketing will help to counter each of these challenges.

First, I'm aware that it's less than ideal to lump all nonprofits into one group. Nonprofits contribute about six percent of the total United States Gross Domestic Product. With about 1.5 million nonprofits registered in the United States, it's a significant sector of the economy.[32] Many, many nonprofits take marketing very seriously and do fantastic marketing work.

The discussion and recommendations in this chapter concern the sizable subset of nonprofit charitable organizations—501(c)(3) organizations—that do need help with their marketing.

## Symptom: The Splintering of Fundraising and Marketing

In Chapter 1, we saw that organizations of all types are suffering from four different symptoms of dysfunction in marketing. A fifth symptom can be

---

[32] Urban Institute. (2020, June 4). *The Nonprofit Sector in Brief 2019*. https://nccs.urban.org/publication/nonprofit-sector-brief-2019

added to the list when considering nonprofit organizations in particular: and that is the splintering of fundraising and marketing.

Whereas in the for-profit world, the vast majority of organizations consider marketing/sales to be the default operating unit responsible for orchestrating the acquisition of revenue, in the nonprofit world that responsibility is carved up into a number of camps—namely: development, advancement, external affairs, marketing, and fundraising.

The underlying cause of the splintering is that nonprofits commonly generate revenue of two general types: earned revenue and contributed revenue. Earned revenue is generated in exchange for goods or services rendered (such as hospital fees, college tuition, or museum admission fees). Contributed revenue comes in the form of outright donations and grants from individuals, foundations and other sources.

The relative importance of earned versus contributed revenue for individual nonprofits varies widely. But in the aggregate, according to the National Council of Nonprofits, 49 percent of the revenue generated by charitable organizations in the United States is earned revenue generated through private sources, 31.8 percent is earned through government grants and contracts, 14 percent comes from donations, and 5.2 percent from other sources.[33] This was not always the case.

In the earliest days of nonprofits in the United States, most revenue was contributed. Therefore, the original model for generating revenue was to seek donations. Consequently, nonprofit organizations were structured around classic fundraising activities. In the mid-twentieth century, things changed when the tax code was updated creating today's tax-exempt public charity, or the 501(c)(3). Since that time, nonprofits have grown exponentially in number and in size. They have also begun to operate more like their for-profit counterparts in terms of how they approach their operations.

One key result of the growth is that, in general, earned revenue has become an increasingly important component of the nonprofit budget while contributed revenue has declined in importance. And as earned revenue be-

---

[33] National Council of Nonprofits. (2019, Fall). *Nonprofit Impact Matters: How America's Charitable Nonprofits Strengthen Communities and Improve Lives.* https://www.nonprofitimpactmatters.org/site/assets/files/1/nonprofit-impact-matters-sept-2019-1.pdf

came more important, nonprofits began engaging in the kinds of marketing activities found in the for-profit world. An important consequence of the dual revenue streams is that we now see a split in responsibility for earned and contributed revenue as evidenced typically by two different organizational departments, each competing for limited resources and each competing for a voice in their leadership circles.

And that's a problem. But it's also an opportunity.

As to the problem, having two units competing for resources isn't unusual in organizations. However, when those separate units are each communicating directly with customers/clients/donors, that competition can create dysfunction because each unit has its own goals to pursue and because each unit has its own ideas regarding the type of language that will potentially drive more revenue. Each unit will have differing ideas regarding the appropriate messaging frequency, and message types. The competing units will very often end up sending competing or conflicting messages out into the world, thereby hindering the nonprofit's ability to generate revenue.

The key here is that your nonprofit might have very good reasons indeed to operate separate units for earned versus contributed revenue. Nevertheless, those units must absolutely be on the same page in terms of messaging. There must be a seamless framework that binds the two departments' messaging because communication bleeds. Your target audiences will overlap to some degree—maybe a great degree. And today's casual customer may soon become a major donor. Individuals on the outside of your organization won't know (or care) if the information they are receiving is coming from your development team or from your marketing team. They'll just know that they are receiving information from your organization. So, the communication must be consistent, coherent and purposeful—if it's to be successful.

As to the opportunity, how can we prevent these two units from getting out of sync? For many organizations, the solution is placing both units under a single VP of External Relations or Advancement. But that will not automatically fix the problem because the splintering isn't something that can simply be fixed by tweaking one's organizational chart.

This is why.

First of all, there exists a remarkably wide range of opinions regarding the proper place for marketing within the nonprofit world. On one end of the spectrum, there are many who view marketing as a patently inappropriate use of a nonprofit's funds. On the other end, there are many organizations where marketing is viewed much the same way as in the for-profit world. Most nonprofit leaders find themselves somewhere between these two poles. The wide range in attitudes further exposes the fact that there is an underlying lack of understanding when it comes to what "marketing" is.

One of marketing's big problems in the nonprofit world is that it is often viewed as shamelessly commercial. This is understandable on one level. After all, the wonderful thing about nonprofits is that they are driven by causes rather than commercialism. And when your organization is pursuing a cause, it feels like every dollar you spend should be applied directly to your cause—whether it's easing the plight of those who are suffering, caring for an important historical asset or collection of artifacts, providing an education, caring for the environment, or supporting the arts. The motivation to steward one's budget is driven by a sense of altruism. Nonetheless, spending money on marketing does not constitute a betrayal of one's mission.

Recall that as discussed in Chapter 3, and contrary to widely held views, marketing writ large isn't about communication—it's about competing. Communication just happens to be the most observable component of marketing. Therefore, people equate marketing with communication. But nonprofits do compete. They compete for philanthropic dollars. They compete for the patronage of visitors and for patients. They compete for students. They compete to raise the awareness of their causes. And the successful pursuit of each of these competitive activities necessitates some form of communication, whether personal, written or digital.

Good communication, as has been stressed throughout this book, doesn't begin and end with an advertising budget and tactics. Good communication begins with an understanding of purpose. With whom are we communicating? What's the message we wish to convey? What other organizations are attempting to communicate a message similar to ours? How can we craft and deliver our message in the most effective manner if our goal is to increase impact, awareness and patronage?

A requirement for effective communication is that it must serve a purpose. Now, one might assume that this is good news for nonprofits because nonprofits live and breathe purpose. However, an ironic problem with nonprofits is that while they do have purposes, which are usually articulated in the form of their mission statements, those mission statements are often missing a few essential ingredients. The missions of most nonprofits are based only upon two things: the organization itself, and the cause the organization is pursuing. Nonprofit missions don't typically place sufficient emphasis on: (a) their competitive environment or (b) their customer.

Think of the competitive environment this way. For example, if your organization's purpose is to put an end to the mistreatment of animals, then it may very well be that the most effective way to serve your purpose is simply to raise money on behalf of PETA or the Humane Society or the ASPCA—competing organizations also committed to improving the treatment of animals. Why start an entirely new organization and duplicate the good work of these other well established nonprofits, right?

The fact is that whatever your nonprofit organization does, there are other organizations doing roughly or even precisely the same thing as yours. Your nonprofit competes. And your organization will struggle needlessly if it doesn't manage its competition thoughtfully.

As is the case with the term "competition," the notion of a "customer" represents another area where nonprofits struggle. Nonprofits are typically formed to meet some type of need with social or community importance. The individuals who benefit directly from the services of nonprofits are not necessarily the organization's customers, however. Think of customers as the individuals who provide you with the resources you need in order to further your organization's mission.

So, with the exception of those organizations whose operations are funded exclusively by permanent endowments, nonprofits are: (a) in the business of serving their community and (b) in the business of securing revenue in order to further their important work in the community.

The point here is that nonprofit mission statements usually focus on service to the community while ignoring the twin need to secure revenue. Nonprofit missions are typically expressed in terms of the organization and what it does for the community. The fact that most nonprofits don't adequately frame their missions with an eye toward their sources of revenue is limiting the effectiveness of their marketing.

The DEEP Marketing process can help nonprofits immensely in this area. Recall that the first step in DEEP Marketing is called Discover (Chapters 4–8). In the Discover process, your organization conducts an analysis of its customer family, its competitive league, and of itself. As a result of the process, your nonprofit organization will gain a much clearer picture of its unique niche in the larger market.

Gaining that perspective is critically important as it will allow your nonprofit to operate with clearer purpose. That clearer purpose will allow you to create clearer communication. And that clearer communication will allow you to connect better with the people who can help support your organization.

In the end, I believe the main reason for the splintering we see in fundraising and marketing in nonprofits is that the notion of "marketing" is misunderstood by so many of us. As we explored in Part 1 of the book, marketing must seep down into every level of any organization. This allows an organization's messaging to connect to everything else the organization does. So whether your particular nonprofit uses the term "advancement" or "external affairs," don't let your taxonomic preferences keep you from generating more revenue.

Nonprofits would do so much better if they apply the DEEP Marketing framework and let it inform everything that their advancement, development, external affairs, fundraising and marketing teams do. On a strategic level, DEEP Marketing can help nonprofits develop a clearer and more accurate sense of their position in the marketplace. DEEP Marketing also helps on a tactical level with every marketing-related activity a nonprofit pursues. Let's look at some examples.

## Using DEEP Marketing to Increase Earned and Contributed Revenue

The end game for marketing in the vast majority of organizations, whether for-profit or nonprofit, is pretty straightforward: connect with individuals (or groups) in order to generate net revenue sustainably. For nonprofits, as we know, revenue is commonly separated into two streams: contributed revenue and earned revenue.

When it comes to contributed revenue, donors and potential donors are being targeted with greater sophistication and by a greater number of nonprofits than ever before. In short, there is a higher degree of competition for those donor dollars. Your nonprofit stands to boost its competitiveness for contributed revenue if it can craft an appeal grounded in a competitively minded framework. So, how do we do that? By addressing those needs in the Discover phase of DEEP Marketing.

Nonprofits must be mindful of the fact that they have a wide number of target audiences when they are conducting their Discover phase. Private donors, corporate donors, foundations, and governmental funders each have their own set of needs. And since their needs are distinct, a nonprofit needs to manage its Discover phase with each target audience in mind. As your organization brings definition to the three constellations making up its competitive environment (Chapters 4–8), it's important you seek out overlaps that will have crossover appeal to each of your audiences. It is important because some nonprofits approach their different target audiences with different appeals.

Applying different communication tactics to reach different target audiences isn't necessarily a problem but the overarching appeal needs to be consistent. Your organization's purpose is the same whether you are engaging with a small donor or one with very deep pockets. So, don't let one specific donor type dominate your findings in the Discover phase at the expense of other donor types. Look for commonalities throughout the process.

In Chapter 8, we learned that in the Discover phase, the goal is to generate a statement describing your organization's superpowers. The desired language was to be framed along the following lines:

> People are suffering because an important need isn't being met very well. Our organization meets this need exceptionally well, and in a way no one else does.

Now, when a nonprofit reads this, they may immediately think that the need they are meeting is the social need they are addressing. For example, a nonprofit focused on feeding the homeless might think their superpower would be worded roughly like this:

> Homeless people are going hungry. Our organization meets this need exceptionally well, and in a way no one else does.

Notice, however, the sentence doesn't reference your customer. It includes your beneficiary, but not your customer. The statement is all about your organization and the social need. With this type of language, customers are left to connect themselves into the equation. This common error misses the entire point of the Discover phase—which is to connect your organization, your competitors, and your customer.

Remember that your customer is defined as the person (or organization) who is paying your organization in exchange for what you offer. And that payment is not strictly in exchange for what you offer your customer, but for what you offer to the community. For what you offer to the world.

This idea is particularly important for nonprofits simply because there are other organizations doing similar work to yours. If your organization ceased to exist, then another organization would most likely step up to fill its shoes. So your organization absolutely must connect itself with its funders if it wishes to have any funders.

Therefore, a preferable way to frame the organization's superpower would be as follows:

> People are frustrated seeing so much food go to waste when there are so many homeless people going hungry every day. Our nonprofit organization was created to up-cycle unsold food from restaurants and grocery stores and deliver it to homeless individuals and families who desperately need it.

As you can see, this statement includes the people who are troubled by the rampant waste of food, and who want to support the organization's creative efforts to address the problem. The issue of hunger is appropriately front and center, but the message is also directed to those who are driven to help. While it may seem counterintuitive to shift the focus in this way, it's vitally important.

Donors pledge their money to nonprofits *like* yours because it makes them feel good to be contributing to a cause that matters to them. But they are pledging their support to your nonprofit *specifically* because they feel your organization will address the cause in a particular manner that feels right to them. There are many other organizations helping the hungry. You need to remind your potential supporters that your nonprofit helps the hungry in a unique way that feels right to them.

The same logic applies to donor organizations as it does to individual donors. Funding organizations want to see their support going to nonprofits that have a distinctive role to play in meeting needs. Like individuals, funding organizations have choices with respect to where they direct their funds. The search for funding is competitive, so your nonprofit needs to have a messaging framework informed by that competitive environment. DEEP Marketing will help your nonprofit reframe its messaging in a way that will enhance its efforts to generate contributed revenue.

Now, when it comes to earned revenue, nonprofit organizations must be careful to stay closely aligned with their chartered missions. There are two reasons for this. First, a nonprofit's tax-exempt status places conditions upon its earned income activities, particularly with respect to income that is unrelated to its mission. Secondly, keeping one's earned income activities aligned closely to one's mission will yield greater and more sustainable revenue. The key question here is: "Which mission?"

When a nonprofit aligns its earned revenue activities with its institutional mission statement, problems are bound to arise. As is the case with contributed revenue, the problems stem from the fact that nonprofit missions aren't typically written with the customer in mind. Nonprofit missions are usually written with a more high-minded purpose—which is understandable.

However, cause-oriented mission statements aren't structured to help guide your organization toward a path of sustainable revenue generation.

The generation of earned revenue begs for a market-oriented platform. In our earlier discussion on contributed revenue, we saw that including the customer in your marketing mission provides a stronger basis for appeals speaking more directly to donors. Similarly, organizations that are more reliant on earned revenue such as those involved in healthcare, the arts, or education can enhance their streams of earned revenue significantly if they realign their public facing activities according to a customer-driven framework.

Reorienting one's marketing mission is easier with respect to earned revenue activities than it is with respect to contributed revenue. Since earned revenue activities involve an exchange of money for goods or services, there is a much clearer customer to keep in mind.

Applying the DEEP Marketing process will allow you to identify how your customer and your competitors dovetail into your mission.

## Using DEEP Marketing to Amplify a Limited Nonprofit Marketing Budget

Nonprofits tend to have an uneasy relationship with marketing in a general sense, so it shouldn't be a surprise that many also have a hard time allocating sufficient funds to support their marketing activities. There are two main reasons for this. First, nonprofits tend to see marketing as an optional activity. Optional, in this case, means that marketing can be funded only if money remains after having met mission-related obligations such as serving the community or caring for a collection. The trap of this type of thinking is that if an activity is viewed as optional, it is likely to be considered unnecessary.

The second factor causing nonprofits to underfund their marketing budgets is the drive to keep administrative costs low. It's a commonly held belief that potential donors are more likely to support a nonprofit whose administrative expenses are low as opposed to one whose expenses are high. The rationale is that if I want to donate my hard-earned money to a nonprofit that feeds the homeless, won't my donation have a greater impact if I support the organization with the lowest administrative expense? I don't want my donation to pay for marketing. I want it to go to food, right? Nonprofit efficiency scores are available online, and—whether justified or not— nonprofits worry that high administrative expenses may potentially suppress their access to contributed capital.

Although there isn't a clear consensus on how significantly efficiency ratings impact giving, the fact remains most nonprofits are working with relatively insecure marketing budgets. As a result, nonprofits should, at a minimum, seek ways to be more efficient with their limited dollars. DEEP Marketing enables nonprofits to do exactly that.

First, consider that there is no shortage of information available to nonprofits seeking to improve their marketing. Free nonprofit marketing advice is plentiful—but the bulk of it is patchy and largely tactical. More importantly, very little advice is available in the form of a holistic framework—which is more likely to yield better results for every dollar spent in marketing.

If you look online for nonprofit marketing advice, you'll find all kinds of reasonable and well-intentioned recommendations such as: "Create customer profiles," or "Take advantage of social media to raise awareness," or "Optimize your nonprofit website for the search engines." These are good bits of advice but they are rather like a list of things to do to improve your health: "Stop smoking, eat better, and get more exercise."

While the advice is useful in the aggregate, it is far too generalized to be useful to me in particular. Besides, what's being advised is something I already, or should already, know. If I want to improve my health, I need a customized plan built around my particular needs and capabilities. The same is true of nonprofit marketing advice online. The majority of the advice doesn't really offer solutions based on what my unique organization needs.

What your nonprofit organization needs in order to market itself well is to apply a framework allowing you to develop and implement tactics tailored specifically to your organization. More importantly though, you shouldn't be jumping straight into tactics. Tactics need to emerge from an underlying strategy. DEEP Marketing provides such footing for your nonprofit. Here are a number of examples showing how DEEP Marketing can improve your nonprofit's marketing.

First of all, the DEEP Marketing framework yields a DEEP Connector. Your DEEP Connector will provide you with the key drivers and language you need given the constraints of your smaller marketing budget. A limited budget requires you to be more deliberate and efficient with your tactics because you have less of an opportunity to correct any communications misfires. In addition, your for-profit competitors are likely to be outspending you. So efficiency and powerful messaging are critical.

The second area of benefit DEEP Marketing provides is in the way your organization approaches the marketing community in search of pro bono (free) help. During many of my years of nonprofit marketing I sought the assistance of marketing agencies who were willing to perform pro bono work for the organizations where I worked. The value my organizations received was absolutely tremendous. But there is a right way and a wrong way to seek pro bono help.

Since great creative work can be very difficult to generate from within your nonprofit organization, and since creative work is what tangibly connects your DEEP Connector with your potential customer, then a creative agency should be the first pro bono partnership for you to nail down. Let's look at how that's done.

The first thing to do when trying to secure pro bono support is to seek out an agency owner (or someone who has an ownership stake) who can connect personally to the work your organization performs in the community. Without a committed principal at your partner organization, you are not likely to get very good or consistent work. With a committed principal, however, you will be opening the door to great work for very little cost. So, the first hurdle to overcome is to secure the right match. And securing the right match means: (a) identifying your potential match and then (b) persuading that potential match to become a committed match.

Finding a potential match comes down to simple networking and outreach. The much harder part is persuading the potential match to become a committed match. A crisp and passionate statement of purpose is precisely what a potentially interested marketing partner needs in order to become convinced. Fortunately, your DEEP Connector provides you with a concise and compelling description of what your organization is all about.

*Nonprofit Organizations*

But I'd like to let you in on a secret. The hidden reason your DEEP Connector will serve you here is that your potential pro bono partner isn't only interested in your mission. Your potential marketing partner is also keenly interested in the quality of work they can do for you. And they are interested in the type of client you are going to be.

I've had a number of pro bono relationships with agencies over the course of my career. In fact, some of the best marketing work I was ever involved with came through these partnerships, even though we were only paying direct costs. The two reasons the relationships were so successful are: very clear direction was provided to the agencies, and the agencies were allowed to stretch their creative muscles.

I've been told by a number of agency owners that running your own agency means you will have two broad types of clients: (a) clients who are a pain to work with, and (b) clients who are a pleasure to work with. Now, before you assume that being a pain to work with means you are just being firm, and before you assume that being a pleasure to work with means you are a pushover, let me elaborate.

Like most of us, the people who own and work for marketing agencies love nothing more than to do great work. They want to create marketing that makes a solid impression and delivers outstanding results for their clients. That's why they work for marketing agencies. It's why they own marketing agencies. Because they love successful marketing. But when you own an agency, a significant number of your clients are going to be a pain to work with. That's just how it is.

Those difficult clients will never be satisfied with creative proposals, yet they won't be able to articulate exactly what they do want, or why they simply "don't like" the concepts they are shown. Those clients will provide conflicting feedback with respect to creative ideas. Those clients, too, will have a hard time sticking with a creative idea long enough to let it take hold. But difficult clients are paying clients, so the agency devotes a lot of time and resources in an attempt to make them happy. The agency has bills to pay, after all.

Keeping all of this in mind, your goal as a pro bono client is to do everything you can to ensure that the people working on your account are thrilled

*191*

with your energy and thrilled with the work they create for you. If they are energized about the success opportunity you provide, and if you have given them very clear expectations, then you may very well be thrilled, too.

Use the DEEP Connector you created in the DEEP Marketing process to demonstrate to your potential pro bono agency that your organization:

- Has a very clear understanding of who your audience is
- Has a very clear understanding as to the message it wishes to convey
- Has a very clear understanding as to who your chief competitors are
- Has a number of communication Pillars needing to be amplified by creative work

In addition, share that your entire team is tightly aligned with respect to the four items listed above. Your aim is to convince the agency owner that you are going to be one of their all-time favorite clients—and not just another one of their challenging clients. It's rather certain if an agency owner believes you are going to be a pain, they won't be too eager to support you, even if they love your cause.

The icing on the cake is that once your partner commits to supporting your nonprofit, you are likely to benefit from additional opportunities for pro bono support because your partner may well go to bat for you. I recall working in one nonprofit where we received world-class creative support, production support and media support to the tune of hundreds of thousands of unbilled dollars. The agency team was so excited to do the work that they were twisting the arms of their production vendors to ensure the ads got created at the absolutely lowest cost possible.

The agency also worked with local TV stations to run the ads as public service announcements (PSAs). While we, the client, couldn't choose what time slots the PSAs would run, we still received a tremendous amount of quality air time. One of the reasons we were able to receive so much free air is that the ads themselves possessed professional production values. They didn't look like your typical produced-on-a-shoestring PSAs.

I was astounded that I could get such incredible creative support with such a strictly limited budget. But it took me years to actually figure out why we were able to achieve it for so many campaigns. It turns out the formula was simple in concept, but not easy in execution. The formula, as I said, was to be very clear up front, and then let the creative folks sink their teeth into the project without me continually derailing the process. It came down to me doing everything I could to be a dream client—one who gets results that both the client and the agency are very proud of.

Plus, it's not like I had a lot of choice in the matter. As a non-paying client, I didn't have the luxury of being a jerk. This is one case where the saying, "You get what you pay for," takes on a twist in meaning. We weren't paying in cash but we were paying in terms of preparation and in terms of a determined openness to creative ideas. And, as a result, we got much more than what we paid for. The agency did as well. Their creative team got to create some really fun, award-winning work and were given the chance to keep loving their jobs while some of their paying clients were making them hate their jobs.

A creative agency is a great first place to try to secure pro bono work—but don't limit the exercise to creative agencies. You can also find digital agencies, media buying agencies and media partners willing to do pro bono work if you can be the kind of client they need. It's a two-way street and nothing will prepare you to be a great client more than having gone through the DEEP Marketing process.

## Using DEEP Marketing to Connect Better With Your Community

Now that we've looked at how DEEP Marketing can help your nonprofit make the most of its limited marketing budget, let's look at how it can impact many of your other non-paid marketing and outreach activities.

First, it's not just your donors and patrons who need to know who you are. Your community needs to know what your organization does and why. The specific goal in this is to get the community to embrace your work and feel that its work is something that makes their community special.

To serve as an example, let's take an in-depth look at how a museum might apply DEEP Marketing in order to connect more authentically with its community. Museums represent just a slice of the nonprofit world. But they provide an example we can all relate to because, like all nonprofits, museums have missions, and they employ familiar mechanisms for generating both contributed and earned revenue.

The key to unlocking your museum's authenticity is found in the Discover phase of DEEP Marketing. In Chapter 7 we learned how to go about discovering your own organization. As one of the three constellations defining an organization's competitive marketplace, your organization's unique attributes and strengths matter tremendously. As a nonprofit organization, you will also possess assets (your collection and your facilities) that have been deemed worthy of special corporate status. Your designation as a 501(c)(3) is a precious thing that can and should be leveraged.

Of course, it's not the actual tax designation that will matter—it's that the designation declares your organization to be an important community asset. Your organization needs to exude its chartered importance because it can connect your nonprofit to the world at large. Recall that the key asset the DEEP framework will provide you with is a DEEP Connector which is meant, among other things, to connect your organization with the community. It is therefore essential your DEEP Connector acknowledges and even celebrates its special connection with the community it serves.

Over the years—both as a museum leader and museum patron—I have learned that the connective tissue binding museums with their communities is authenticity. It is similar in the business world but with museums, authenticity just seems to matter more. I'm aware that authenticity can be defined in many ways. So, what I mean by authenticity is the extent to which a museum is in touch with and able to express: (a) why its unique collection matters, and (b) why the manner and place in which it is being presented lends uncommon meaning to the collection.

Authenticity is a pathway to building deeper emotional connections between a community and a museum. And deeper emotional connections translate to greater revenue for museums in terms of membership, contributions, retail, and events.

But that greatly needed revenue is simply an outgrowth of what matters more. The deep connection museums can build with their communities should be an echo of the connection the original collector has (or had) with their collection. If museum professionals are driven by these authentic interpersonal connections, then revenue will be far easier to generate.

## Step 1: Why Does Your Collection Matter?

Reflect on your collection and pinpoint why it matters to an ordinary person (as opposed to a museum professional). We all collect things. We begin collecting things as children. Everyone can connect with the mystique and excitement of a collection and to a collector's desire to shape, preserve and share the collection.

Your museum's collection, too, has a mystique—or a story that has importance to your community. So the first step is to illuminate what the story is. Make certain the Narrative in your DEEP Connector conveys the story, and make sure it does not read like everyone else's story. Your collection may be similar to that of other museums, but the telling of its story must be unique if it is to be compelling.

## Step 2: How Do Your Museum's Facilities and Location Lend Special Meaning to Your Collection?

Museums know well that people visit in order to see their collection(s) as well as to see their facility. A museum visit is an experience melding content and place. This is why so many museums are based in exciting buildings or designed by superstar architects. Like it or not, curators, many people want to visit an I. M. Pei or Frank Gehry building even more than they care about what's inside. The key question is: "How do you meaningfully connect the inside with the outside?"

So, for example, an air and space museum situated on an active and historic airfield should be able to provide tremendous context for the story of its collection. This is not to say that a historic building in a city center could not also provide distinctive context for an air and space museum. The point is that you have to flesh out your context and make it apparent to your audience. Visitors want meaning. They want to share that meaning. So, help them understand the meaning.

## Step 3: Extend the Meaning You Have Discovered in Steps 1 and 2 Into Everything Else Your Museum Does

Does a visitor entering your museum's retail space feel like they have somehow stepped into an airport bookstore? I hope not—even though it is the case for most museums. Visitors are far less likely to continue enjoying their visit in your store if they feel removed from the museum's magic embrace. Allow your visitor to fully enjoy their retail experience by helping them connect it to all the amazing work you've created in your gallery spaces.

To illustrate, I served as project manager for a museum store remodel that transformed a traditional retail environment into an immersive one. Ceiling and lighting treatments, floors and fixtures in the new space were all designed to work together to reflect the stories in the museum's galleries. The transformation resulted in visitors spending more money while simultaneously helping the retail staff feel more connected to the museum's collection and mission.

The same idea applies to your catering or event spaces. Allow all your spaces to be part of the story—not to overwhelm—but to connect them meaningfully and authentically. Every visitor to your facility should feel as if they are being invited to make that connection to your amazing story.

Authenticity takes time to build. Following these steps will take time. It will take a lot of thought and work to tackle each of the steps above. But the investment will pale in comparison to the value that you realize in the future.

♦ ♦ ♦ ♦

Whether your nonprofit is dedicated to the arts or to human services or education or anything else, the DEEP Marketing framework can help you reframe its purpose in order to gain a clearer understanding of its role in the

## Nonprofit Organizations

community. As a result, nonprofits can extract far greater value from limited marketing budgets, and connect more authentically with sources of funding, and with their community. As such, DEEP Marketing is a proven process that can be exceedingly fruitful for nonprofit organizations.

# About the Author

Bill Hayes is the creator of the DEEP Marketing framework. During his career, Bill has held marketing leadership roles at several museums and universities in the Seattle area. In 2019, Bill and his wife traveled throughout Mexico for half a year before relocating to the San Diego area, where he started Iceberg Marketing Consulting in 2020. During the pandemic, Bill completed his first book, *DEEP Marketing*.

Bill's professional passion is helping the leaders of organizations discover and embrace their ideal position in the market.

Please feel free to send your feedback or questions to:
Bill Hayes, Iceberg Marketing Consulting
bill@icebergmc.com

Made in the USA
Columbia, SC
07 October 2023